THE HAMMER

Why Dogs Attack Us and How to Prevent It

Bryan Bailey

Praise for *Embracing the Wild in Your Dog*

"This book represents much more than a simple training guide. There is an undeniable power and beauty to the author's musings as he weaves into the text vital lessons learned from his mentor during intense survival training in the Alaskan wilderness. A firm response to currently accepted dog training methods."

~ Kirkus Reviews

"Rarely does a book come along that so positively mesmerizes me that I read it from start to finish in a single sitting. Yet that is exactly what I did with Embracing the Wild in Your Dog by Bryan Bailey. Bailey's work is truly worthy of the attention of others and, in my estimation, of an award or two! If you are a dog owner, this one is definitely worth your while."

~ Patricia Reding, Reader's Favorite Reviewer and Award Winning Author

"Overall, Embracing the Wild in Your Dog is captivating, well-written, and very informative. It allows people to come to a better understanding of dog behaviors, how dogs originate from the wolf, and why they continue to portray many of the same survival mannerisms today. It also points out how our misperception of our pet dog as a small, furry human is completely incorrect."

~ Portland Book Review

"Embracing the Wild in Your Dog is a wealth of insight from a vastly experienced dog trainer. While not a training manual, when setting out to train your own 'puppy pal' or 'furbaby', this is a valuable book to help you to perhaps understand why your dog loves your kids, but goes berserk when the neighbor boy shows up."

~ Manhattan Book Review

Other Books by the Author

Embracing the Wild in Your Dog
Housebreaking - 10 Steps to Success

For The Victims of Canine Aggression

Date of Death	Name	Age
August 26, 2017	Alicia Malagon	76 years old
August 19, 2017	Michael Obergas	2 months old
August 6, 2017	"John Doe"	3 weeks old
August 2, 2017	William Gamble	66 years old
August 1, 2017	Paris Adams	20 months old
July 27, 2017	Jacob Brooks	4 years old
July 21, 2017	Michael Parks	60 years old
July 11, 2017	Vinson Tucker	79 years old
June 25, 2017	Melissa Barnes	65 years old
June 9, 2017	Marcos Raya, Jr.	18 months old
June 1, 2017	Margaret Colvin	90 years old
May 26, 2017	Susannah Murray	3 weeks old
May 12, 2017	Sandra Keiser	71 years old
May 8, 2017	Kamiko Tsuda-Saelee	6 months old
April 27, 2017	Lisa Green	32 years old
April 25, 2017	Maurice Brown	60 years old
April 6, 2017	Cecille Short	82 years old
March 23, 2017	Jase Ohs	8 months old
February 27, 2017	Valentine Herrera	76 years old
February 24, 2017	James Bennett	79 years old
February 16, 2017	"John Doe"	5 years old
February 13, 2017	Louise Hermida	75 years old
January 17, 2017	Skylar Julius	2 months old
January 17, 2017	Logan Braatz	6 years old
December 16, 2016	David Fear	64 years old

Date of Death	Name	Age
December 2, 2016	Isaiah Jacob Franklin	6 years old
October 25, 2016	Daisie Bradshaw	68 years old
October 23, 2016	Kiyana McNeal	4 years old
September 24, 2016	Piper Nevaeh Dunbar	2 years old
September 1, 2016	Baby Jane Doe	6 days old
August 29, 2016	Susan Shawl	60 years old
August 19, 2016	Michael Downing	83 years old
August 17, 2016	Derion Stevenson	9 years old
August 1, 2016	Michelle Wilcox	30 years old
July 29, 2016	Crisencio Aliado	52 years old
July 16, 2016	Elizabeth Rivera	71 years old
July 14, 2016	Kayden Colter Begay	3 years old
June 27, 2016	Susie Kirby	3 days old
June 20, 2016	Jocelyn Winfrey	53 years old
June 15, 2016	Erin McCleskey	36 years old
June 4, 2016	Hunter Bragg	7 years old
June 4, 2016	Earl Wayne Stephens, Jr.	43 years old
May 10, 2016	Adonis Reddick	45 years old
May 9, 2016	Antoinette Brown	52 years old
April 24, 2016	Manuel Mejia	49 years old
April 21, 2016	Sebastian Caban	3 days old
April 14, 2016	Valente Lopez Aguirre	58 years old
March 31, 2016	Sonda Dyan Tyson	66 years old
March 28, 2016	Bessie Flowers	84 years old
March 8, 2016	Gladys Alexander	92 years old
February 11, 2016	Suzanne Story	36 years old
February 7, 2016	Aiden Grim	3 days old
January 24, 2016	Talan West	7 years old
January 8, 2016	Payton Sawyers	15 months old
January 3, 2016	Tyler Trammell-Huston	9 years old
December 20, 2015	Nyjah Espinosa	2 years old
December 16, 2015	Maria Torres	57 years old
December 4, 2015	Werner Vogt	85 years old
December 3, 2015	Rebecca Hardy	22 years old
December 2, 2015	Xavier Strickland	4 years old
November 15, 2015	Carter Hartle	11 months old
November 12, 2015	Anthony Riggs	57 years old
November 8, 2015	Amiyah Dunston	9 years old
October 18, 2015	Tanner Smith	5 years old

Date of Death	Name	Age
October 16, 2015	Edgar Brown	60 years old
September 28, 2015	Lamarkus Hicks	2 years old
September 22, 2015	Carmen Reigada	91 years old
September 8, 2015	Emilio Rios	65 years old
September 4, 2015	Barbara McCormick	65 years old
August 24, 2015	Cathy H. Wheatcraft	48 years old
August 22, 2015	Porsche Cartee	25 years old
August 10, 2015	Max Gracia	25 years old
July 24, 2015	Carolyn Lamp	67 years old
July 12, 2015	Annie Williams	71 years old
July 7, 2015	Joshua Strother	6 years old
July 2, 2015	Norberto Legarda	83 years old
June 28, 2015	Jordan Collins-Tyson	3 years old
May 25, 2015	James Nevils, III	5 years old
May 24, 2015	Anthony Wind	26 years old
May 2, 2015	Gaege Ramirez	7 days old
April 19, 2015	Brayden Wilson	10 weeks old
April 14, 2015	Kenneth Ford	79 years old
March 31, 2015	Neta Lee Adams	81 years old
March 21, 2015	De'Trick Johnson	38 years old
March 14, 2015	Julia Charging Whirlwind	49 years old
March 12, 2015	Betty Wood	78 years old
March 8, 2015	Roy Higgenbotham, Jr.	63 years old
February 22, 2015	TayLynn DeVaughn	2 years old
February 4, 2015	Fredrick Crutchfield	63 years old
January 22, 2015	Malaki Mildward	7 years old
January 19, 2015	Declan Moss	18 months old
January 7, 2015	Eugene Smith	87 years old
December 25, 2014	Edward Cahill	40 years old
December 15, 2014	Rita Ross Woodard	64 years old
December 6, 2014	Christopher J. Camejo	2 years old
December 1, 2014	Bobbie Cheveallier	85 years old
November 23, 2014	Jose Cruz Cazares Robles	62 years old
November 18, 2014	Jayla Rodriguez	8 years old
November 14, 2014	Stella Antanaitis	91 years old
November 12, 2014	Deanne Lynn Coando	40 years old
October 25, 2014	Alemeaner Dial	83 years old
October 24, 2014	Logan Meyer	7 years old
October 15, 2014	Juan Fernandez	54 years old

Date of Death	Name	Age
September 26, 2014	Alice Payne	75 years old
September 20, 2014	David Glass, Sr.	50 years old
August 13, 2014	Javon Dade, Jr.	4 years old
August 11, 2014	Deriah Solem	22 months old
August 7, 2014	Joel Chirieleison	6 years old
August 4, 2014	Cindy Whisman	59 years old
July 20, 2014	Johnathan Quarles, Jr.	7 months old
July 20, 2014	Logan Shepard	4 years old
June 23, 2014	Craig Sytsma	46 years old
June 9, 2014	Holden Garrison	10 weeks old
May 25, 2014	Rita Pepe	93 years old
May 7, 2014	Kasii Haith	4 years old
May 4, 2014	Nyhiem Wilfong	1 year old
May 3, 2014	Katie Morrison	20 years old
April 28, 2014	Jessica Norman	33 years old
April 11, 2014	Petra Aguirre	83 years old
April 6, 2014	John Harvard	5 years old
April 1, 2014	Dorothy Hamilton	85 years old
March 31, 2014	Christopher Malone	3 years old
March 25, 2014	Mia DeRouen	4 years old
March 14, 2014	Nancy Newberry	77 years old
March 1, 2014	Raymane Robinson, Jr.	2 years old
February 28, 2014	Kenneth Santilla	13 years old
February 26, 2014	Summer Sears	4 years old
February 24, 2014	Braelynn Rayne Coulter	3 years old
February 17, 2014	Je'vaeh Mayes	2 years old
February 7, 2014	Klonda S. Richey	57 years old
January 26, 2014	Annabell Martin	89 years old
January 17, 2014	Kara Hartrich	4 years old
January 6, 2014	Betty Clark	74 years old
January 5, 2014	Christine Bell	43 years old
December 28, 2013	Thomas J. Vick	64 years old
December 13, 2013	Michal Nelson	41 years old
December 10, 2013	Mia Gibson	3 months old
December 7, 2013	Jah'Niyah White	2 years old
November 21, 2013	Joan Kappen	75 years old
November 8, 2013	Levi Watson	4 years old
November 5, 2013	Nga Woodhead	65 years old

Date of Death	Name	Age
November 4, 2013	Katherine Atkins	25 years old
November 1, 2013	Terry Douglass	56 years old
September 27, 2013	Jordan Ryan	5 years old
September 23, 2013	Samuel Eli Zamudio	2 years old
September 22, 2013	Daniel Teubner	2 years old
September 15, 2013	Jordan Reed	5 years old
August 30, 2013	Juan Campos	96 years old
July 1, 2013	Linda Oliver	63 years old
June 25, 2013	Arianna Jolee Merrbach	5 years old
June 17, 2013	Nephi Selu	6 years old
June 9, 2013	Ayden Evans	5 years old
May 12, 2013	Carlton Freeman	80 years old
May 9, 2013	Pamela Marie Devitt	63 years old
April 30, 2013	Rachael Honabarger	35 years old
April 24, 2013	Beau Rutledge	2 years old
April 22, 2013	Jordyn Arndt	4 years old
April 11, 2013	Claudia Gallardo	38 years old
April 7, 2013	Tyler Jett	7 years old
March 27, 2013	Monica Renee Laminack	21 months old
March 6, 2013	Daxton Borchardt	14 months old
March 2, 2013	Ryan Maxwell	7 years old
February 16, 2013	Isaiah Aguilar	2 years old
February 8, 2013	Elsie Grace	91 years old
January 19, 2013	Christian Gormanous	4 years old
January 8, 2013	Betty Todd	65 years old
December 26, 2012	Tomas Henio	8 years old
December 13, 2012	Savannah Edwards	2 years old
December 11, 2012	Elizabeth Hirt	93 years old
December 11, 2012	Esteban Alavez	34 years old
November 14, 2012	Dawn Brown	44 years old
November 11, 2012	Remedios Romeros-Solares	30 years old
November 9, 2012	Dixie Jennings	3 months old
October 18, 2012	Robert Rochester, Jr.	55 years old
October 4, 2012	Tarilyn Bowles	3 weeks old
October 2, 2012	Mary Jo Hunt	54 years old
September 26, 2012	Nellie Davis	60 years old
September 24, 2012	Rayden Bruce	3 months old
September 20, 2012	William Donald Thomas	82 years old
September 11, 2012	James Hudson	10 months old

Date of Death	Name	Age
September 7, 2012	Debra Wilson - Roberts	45 years old
September 5, 2012	Bryton Cason	4 years old
September 1, 2012	Dawn Jurgens	76 years old
August 16, 2012	Charles Hagerman	44 years old
August 12, 2012	Rebecca Carey	23 years old
July 12, 2012	Millicent Miller	82 years old
July 11, 2012	Ronnel Brown	40 years old
June 27, 2012	Kevin Latz	50 years old
June 14, 2012	Tyzhel L. McWilliams	8 months old
June 13, 2012	Jack Redin	2 years old
May 27, 2012	Ja'Marr Tiller	2 years old
May 26, 2012	Eugene Cameron	65 years old
May 17, 2012	Makayla Darnell	3 days old
May 12, 2012	Maryann Hanula	73 years old
May 8, 2012	Jazilyn Mesa	15 months old
May 2, 2012	Clifford Wright	72 years old
April 27, 2012	Jeremiah Eskew-Shahan	1 year old
April 20, 2012	Aiden McGrew	2 months old
April 9, 2012	James Hurst	92 years old
March 25, 2012	Kylar Johnson	4 years old
March 9, 2012	Dylan Andres	17 months old
March 4, 2012	Diane Jansen	59 years old
February 16, 2012	Howard Nicholson, Jr.	2 days old
January 30, 2012	Steven Robertson	6 years old
January 14, 2012	Jace Valdez	23 months old
December 31, 2011	Mable McCallister	84 years old
December 24, 2011	Emako Mendoza	75 years old
December 8, 2011	Misti Wyno	40 years old
December 6, 2011	Tonia Parks	39 years old
December 5, 2011	Joseph Hines	58 years old
November 11, 2011	Edna Dyson	71 years old
October 3, 2011	Mya Maria Maeda	11 days old
September 30, 2011	Nevaeh Bryant	20 months old
September 16, 2011	Donna Conrad	71 years old
September 4, 2011	Brayden McCollen	2 weeks old
August 30, 2011	Carmen Ramos	50 years old
August 30, 2011	Addyson Paige Camerino	9 days old
August 23, 2011	Michael Cook	61 years old
August 12, 2011	James Dowling	4 years old

Date of Death	Name	Age
August 11, 2011	Darla Napora	32 years old
July 3, 2011	Michael Naglee	11 months old
June 29, 2011	Salvador Cotto	6 months old
June 15, 2011	Roy McSweeney	74 years old
June 11, 2011	David Haigler	38 years old
May 29, 2011	Jesse Porter	89 years old
May 27, 2011	Jayelin Graham	4 years old
April 24, 2011	Margaret Salcedo	48 years old
April 22, 2011	Virgil Cantell	50 years old
April 12, 2011	Annabelle Mitchell	7 months old
March 7, 2011	Vanessa Husmann	3 years old
March 6, 2011	Jennie Erquiaga	47 years old
February 19, 2011	Darius Tillman	15 days old
February 17, 2011	Sirlinda Hayes	66 years old
January 26, 2011	Howard James Paul	76 years old
January 26, 2011	Ronnie Waldo	51 years old
January 24, 2011	Kristen Dutton	9 years old
January 12, 2011	Makayla Woodard	5 years old
January 4, 2011	Linda Leal	51 years old
December 19, 2010	Janet Vaughan	3 months old
December 8, 2010	Larry Armstrong	55 years old
December 5, 2010	Edward Mitchell	67 years old
November 16, 2010	Justin Lane	25 years old
November 15, 2010	Shirley Lou Bird	79 years old
November 15, 2010	Cason Bryant	5 years old
November 10, 2010	Kaden Muckleroy	2 years old
November 2, 2010	Christina Casey	53 years old
October 24, 2010	Justin Valentin	4 days old
October 13, 2010	Rev. John Reynolds, Sr.	84 years old
September 4, 2010	Mattie Daugherty	85 years old
August 25, 2010	Taylor Becker	4 years old
August 25, 2010	Jason Walter	7 years old
August 22, 2010	Jerry Yates	69 years old
August 19, 2010	Tracey Payne	46 years old
July 31, 2010	Aaron Carlson	2 years old
July 22, 2010	Jacob Bisbee	2 years old
July 20, 2010	William Parker	71 years old
July 12, 2010	Kyle Holland	5 years old

Date of Death	Name	Age
June 15, 2010	Michael Winters	30 years old
June 3, 2010	Savannah Gragg	9 years old
May 28, 2010	Nathan Aguirre	2 years old
May 25, 2010	Hao Yun "Eddie" Lin	33 years old
May 20, 2010	Krystal Brink	3 years old
April 14, 2010	Thomas Carter, Jr.	7 days old
March 8, 2010	Justin Lopez	9 months old
March 4, 2010	Ethel Horton	65 years old
February 28, 2010	Ashlynn Anderson	4 years old
February 23, 2010	"Jane Doe" Garrett	5 days old
February 20, 2010	Violet Serenity Haaker	3 years old
February 20, 2010	Christine Staab	38 years old
February 19, 2010	Kenneth Bock	57 years old
February 18, 2010	Robert D. Hocker	11 days old
February 12, 2010	Anastasia Bingham	6 years old
February 8, 2010	Carolyn Baker	63 years old
January 17, 2010	Johnny Wilson	56 years old
January 9, 2010	Omar Martinez	3 years old
December 22, 2009	Liam Peck	2 years old
December 12, 2009	Theresa Ellerman	49 years old
December 12, 2009	Dallas Walters	20 months old
December 4, 2009	Lowell Bowden	70 years old
November 30, 2009	Rosie Humphreys	85 years old
November 24, 2009	Karen Gillespie	53 years old
November 5, 2009	Destiny Knox	16 months old
October 28, 2009	Matthew C. "Booter" Hurt	2 years old
October 23, 2009	Colten Smith	17 months old
August 15, 2009	Jasmine Deane	23 months old
August 15, 2009	Justin Kummer	3 days old
August 14, 2009	Lothar Schweder	77 years old
August 14, 2009	Sherry Schweder	65 years old
August 10, 2009	Carter Delaney	20 years old
July 26, 2009	Kathleen J. Doyle	90 years old
June 27, 2009	Gabrial Mandrell-Sauerhage	3 years old
June 15, 2009	Justin Clinton	10 years old
May 11, 2009	Barbara Chambers	59 years old
April 22, 2009	Leonard Lovejoy, Jr.	11 months old
April 13, 2009	David Whitenack, Jr.	41 years old

Date of Death	Name	Age
April 10, 2009	Gordon Lykins	48 years old
April 10, 2009	Michael Landry	4 years old
March 31, 2009	Izaiah Cox	7 months old
March 26, 2009	Tyson Miller	2 years old
March 22, 2009	Dustin Faulkner	3 years old
March 21, 2009	Dolly Newell	80 years old
March 16, 2009	Hill Williams	38 years old
March 4, 2009	"Jane Doe"	2 weeks old
January 19, 2009	Brianna Shanor	8 years old
January 19, 2009	Olivia Rozek	3 weeks old
January 15, 2009	Brooklynn Milburn	4 years old
January 11, 2009	Alex Angulo	4 years old
January 6, 2009	Cheyenne Peppers	5 years old
December 19, 2008	Gerald Adelmund	60 years old
November 26, 2008	Alexander Adams	2 years old
October 31, 2008	Chester Jordan	62 years old
October 5, 2008	Iokepa Liptak	13 months old
September 26, 2008	Katya Todesco	5 years old
September 22, 2008	Kylie Mae Daum	3 days old
September 12, 2008	Cenedi Kia Carey	4 months old
September 9, 2008	Alexis Hennessy	6 days old
September 4, 2008	Luna McDaniel	83 years old
August 17, 2008	Henry Piotrowski	90 years old
August 14, 2008	Isis Krieger	6 years old
August 14, 2008	Robert Howard	35 years old
July 28, 2008	Zane Earles	2 months old
July 25, 2008	Addison Sonney	14 months old
July 22, 2008	Tony Evans, Jr.	3 years old
June 28, 2008	Lorraine May	74 years old
June 18, 2008	Pablo Lopez (Hernandez)	5 years old
May 18, 2008	Tanner Joshua Monk	7 years old
May 14, 2008	Julian Slack	3 years old
April 28, 2008	Abraham Tackett	23 months old
January 20, 2008	Kelli Chapman	24 years old
January 17, 2008	Justin Mozer	6 weeks old
January 4, 2008	Andrew Stein	8 months old
December 25, 2007	Kelly Caldwell	45 years old
December 17, 2007	Blanche Brodeur	76 years old
December 13, 2007	Holden Jernigan	2 years old

Date of Death	Name	Age
December 4, 2007	Cora Lee Suehead	61 years old
November 12, 2007	Jennifer Lowe	21 years old
November 7, 2007	Seth Lovitt	11 years old
November 5, 2007	Tori Whitehurst	4 years old
October 15, 2007	Rosalie Bivens	65 years old
October 5, 2007	"Jane Doe"	73 years old
October 2, 2007	Tina Canterbury	42 years old
September 25, 2007	Karson Gilroy	2 years old
September 13, 2007	Edward Gierlach	91 years old
September 13, 2007	Cheryl Harper	56 years old
September 12, 2007	Kylie Cox	4 months old
August 31, 2007	Scott Warren	6 years old
August 18, 2007	Elijah Rackley	15 months old
August 16, 2007	Zachary King, Jr.	7 years old
July 29, 2007	Saben Jones-Abbott	6 years old
July 23, 2007	Trey Paeth	11 months old
July 12, 2007	Tiffany Pauley	5 years old
June 29, 2007	Mary Bernal	63 years old
June 17, 2007	Phyllis Carroll	63 years old
May 26, 2007	Dandre Fisher	3 years old
May 26, 2007	Carshena Benjamin	71 years old
May 25, 2007	Magdalena Silva	95 years old
May 18, 2007	Celestino Rangel	90 years old
May 17, 2007	James Chapple, Jr.	58 years old
April 23, 2007	Brian Palmer	2 years old
March 22, 2007	Carolina Sotelo	2 years old
March 16, 2007	Pamela Rushing	50 years old
February 16, 2007	Robynn Banks	2 years old
January 28, 2007	Taylor Kitlica	18 months old
January 24, 2007	Matthew Johnson	6 years old
January 15, 2007	Linda Mittino	69 years old
January 12, 2007	Amber Jones	10 years old
November 21, 2006	Pedro Rios	4 years old
November 13, 2006	James Eisaman	40 years old
November 9, 2006	Richard Adams	47 years old
November 6, 2006	Louis Romero, Jr.	2 years old
November 4, 2006	Allen Young	22 months old
November 3, 2006	John Matthew Davis	10 years old
November 3, 2006	Ariel Pogue	2 years old

Date of Death	Name	Age
October 29, 2006	David McCurry	41 years old
October 8, 2006	Jeannine Fusco	44 years old
October 3, 2006	Julius Graham	2 years old
August 29, 2006	Pablo Flietes	52 years old
August 29, 2006	Frank Baber	49 years old
August 18, 2006	Shawna Willey	30 years old
July 31, 2006	John Brannaman	81 years old
July 27, 2006	Jimmie McConnell	71 years old
July 25, 2006	Mariah Puga	3 years old
July 18, 2006	Brandon Coleman	25 years old
July 17, 2006	Sandra Piovesan	50 years old
June 22, 2006	Gemma Carlos	2 years old
June 17, 2006	Javlyin Anderson	15 months old
June 7, 2006	Shaun McCafferty	27 years old
May 11, 2006	Raymond Tomco	78 years old
May 6, 2006	Dianna Acklen	60 years old
May 2, 2006	Juan Garcia	53 years old
April 10, 2006	"John Doe"	unknown
March 20, 2006	Quillan Cottrell	3 years old
March 14, 2006	Charles Gilbert Dalton	52 years old
February 24, 2006	Dominic Giordano	4 years old
February 4, 2006	Conner Lourens	7 years old
January 24, 2006	Kaitlyn Hassard	6 years old
January 9, 2006	Ashton Lee Scott	11 months old
December 30, 2005	Cody Adair	4 years old
December 6, 2005	Mary Stiles	91 years old
November 26, 2005	Lillian Stiles	76 years old
November 24, 2005	Roberto Aguilera	64 years old
November 18, 2005	Hulon Barbour	60 years old
November 6, 2005	Kylee Johnson	14 months old
November 3, 2005	Mike Gomez	86 years old
October 15, 2005	Sydney Akin	6 years old
October 3, 2005	Jonathan Martin	2 years old
August 2, 2005	Cassandra Garcia	16 months old
July 13, 2005	Alexis McDermott	7 days old
July 6, 2005	Dazavious Williams	5 weeks old
July 1, 2005	Boyd Fiscus	83 years old
June 3, 2005	Nicholas Faibish	12 years old

Date of Death	Name	Age
May 17, 2005	Arianna Fleeman	2 years old
May 15, 2005	Julia Beck	87 years old
May 10, 2005	Lorinze Reddings	42 years old
May 7, 2005	Kate-Lynn Logel	7 years old
May 6, 2005	Samantha Black	2 years old
May 2, 2005	Asia Turner	4 years old
April 24, 2005	Ernie Assad	82 years old
April 14, 2005	Laverne Ford	73 years old
April 10, 2005	Robert Schafer	4 years old
April 4, 2005	Cassidy Jeter	6 years old
March 15, 2005	Sandra Sanchez	32 years old
March 8, 2005	Dorothy Sullivan	82 years old
February 4, 2005	Barbara Pilkington	70 years old
January 27, 2005	Lydia Chaplin	14 years old
January 2, 2005	Tyler Babcock	6 years old
December 28, 2004	Florence Morris	78 years old
December 13, 2004	Annilee McKinnon	5 years old
December 13, 2004	Kamryn Billingsly	1 month old
December 10, 2004	Myles Leakes	4 years old
October 8, 2004	Anton Brown	8 years old
October 5, 2004	Jose Diaz	5 weeks old
September 1, 2004	Isaiah Calandis Smith	19 months old
August 6, 2004	Mary DeLacy	87 years old
July 15, 2004	Jordan Lee Parker	8 months old
July 15, 2004	Patricia Anderson	2 years old
July 23, 2004	baby "John Doe"	6 months old
July 27, 2004	Ryker Schweitzer	7 years old
May 31, 2004	Leta Ward	65 years old
April 24, 2004	John Streeter	8 years old
April 19, 2004	Alyssa Villanueva	15 months old
April 16, 2004	Roddie Dumas, Jr.	8 years old
April 3, 2004	baby "John Doe"	16 months old
March 31, 2004	Samuel Trucks	2 years old
March 11, 2004	Madison Carson	2 years old
February 21, 2004	Truston Heart Liddle	17 months old
January 13, 2004	Nathan Roy Hill	3 years old
December 26, 2003	Florence Morris	78 years old
December 12, 2003	Alice Broome	81 years old
November 20, 2003	Jennifer Brooke	40 years old

Date of Death	Name	Age
October 2, 2003	Makayla Paige Sinclair	2 years old
September 7, 2003	Valerie DeSwart	67 years old
August 31, 2003	Isaiah Alley	6 years old
August 2003	Samantha Grace Bauld	3 years old
August 8, 2003	Terry Allen, Jr.	2 weeks old
June 20, 2003	Somer Clugston	2 years old
May 23, 2003	Cedric Edmonds	37 years old
May 16, 2003	Bonnie Page	75 years old
April 2003	Andre Angel Thomas	13 months old
March 26, 2003	Vivian Anthony	54 years old
March 24, 2003	Tre'sean Forsman	3 years old
March 7, 2003	Jennifer Nicole Davis	5 years old
March 2003	Wesley Swindler	3 years old
March 2003	Lily Krajewski	2 years old
February 21, 2003	Alfred Macuk	72 years
December 2002	infant "Jane Doe"	2 weeks old
November 2002	Michael Caylan Garner	5 years old
October 2002	infant "Jane Doe"	23 months old
August 2002	CharLee Shepherd	21 months old
June 1, 2002	Colter Kumpost	4 years old
April 2002	Zachary Grant	2 years old
April 2002	Victoria Morales	5 years old
February 14, 2002	Alicia Clark	10 years old
February 7, 2002	Genoe Novak	6 years old
December 1, 2001	Tristen Gambrel	3 years old
November 20, 2001	Josie Simone Hearon	3 weeks old
November 16, 2001	Alexander J. Bennett	3 days old
October 29, 2001	Kristin Ann Jolley	1 year old
August 21, 2001	Sierra Clayton	3 years old
August 19, 2001	Donald B. Shumpert	2 years old
July 2001	James Dehoyos	2 years old
July 2001	Mathew Cummings	2 years old
June 2001	Mike Copeland	2 years old
June 11, 2001	Tyran Moniz-Hilderbrand	18 months old
June 9, 2001	Kyle Anthony Ross	5 years old
April 30, 2001	Jovanna King	1 month old
April 15, 2001	Willard Kirsh, Jr.	59 years old
April 2001	Mackenzie Madera	5 years old
March 6, 2001	Rodney McAllister	10 years old

Date of Death	Name	Age
March 6, 2001	Joshua Brown	3 years old
March 5, 2001	"Jane Doe" Small	infant
January 26, 2001	Diane Whipple	33 years old
October 7, 2000	infant "Jane Doe"	6 weeks old
September 2000	Ahleah Austin	3 years old
July 2000	Jonathan French	8 years old
June 2000	Jasmine Dillashaw	18 days old
June 2000	Dorothy Stewart	71 years old
May 2000	Quentin Wright	2 years old
April 2000	Ramani Virgil	2 years old
April 2000	Cash Carson	10 years old
March 2000	Dallas Isham	2 years old
February 2000	Josiah Holden	5 years old
February 2000	Daryl Sanders	8 years old
February 2000	Justin Tabner	5 years old
October 1999	Demetrius M. Tucker, Jr.	5 days old
August 1999	Malcolm Morelock	2 years old
July 1999	Melissa Hunt	5 years old
June 1999	Shalen Darshea Cammon	3 years old
March 1999	Darrel Roberson	42 years old
March 1999	Tyler Dean Teter-Chilton	2 weeks old
February 3, 1999	Ellyssa Rhae Peterson	5 years old
February 1999	Jesus Gasca	8 years old
February 1999	Roger Eugene Dukes	6 years old
February 1999	Fily Araujo	2 years old
September 1998	Jordan Schwarze	8 years old
January 1998	Tina Piraino	9 years old
December 1997	April Edwards	5 years old
August 1997	Jonathan Langford	7 years old
July 8, 1997	Salvatore Biagini	70 years old
April 1997	Derrick Brandell	4 years old
April 1997	Christopher Wilson	11 years old
October 1996	Corey Hines	10 years old
July 1996	Kassandra Duvall	21 months old
July 4, 1996	Matthew Pedercini	1 year old
June 1996	John Young	8 years old
March 1996	"Jane Doe"	86 years old
February 1996	Anthony Hunt	4 years old
November 17, 1995	Alec Balbachan	4 years old

Date of Death	Name	Age
October 20, 1995	Walter Feser	75 years old
October 1995	Melton Earl Smith	60 years old
September 1995	Jeffrey Marshall Allen	7 years old
September 1995	Sara Beth Wilkenson	2 weeks old
July 1995	Jessica Hull	1 year old
May 1995	Kirby Lawrence	2 years old
May 19, 1995	Robert A. Thorpe	11 years old
April 1995	Lindsay Shanaman	2 years old
January 1995	Unknown boy	2 years old
November 1994	Baby "Doe" Garcia	infant
September 9, 1994	Anna Claudio	66 years old
February 1994	Tevin Williams	2 years old
January 1994	Amarillys Torres	2 months old
December 1993	Kevin Michael Lahey	2 years old
December 1993	"John Doe"	6 years old
July 1993	Luis Gordo Hernandez	2 years old
May 14, 1993	William Sheppard	2 years old
September 1992	Angela Kaplan	28 years old
June 20, 1992	Daniel Worley	6 years old
May 9, 1992	Randall Ayers	2 years old
February 22, 1992	Derrick Goree	2 years old
February 12, 1992	Robert Coffman	9 months old
February 1992	Jonathan C. Williams	7 years old
November 2, 1991	David Swaine	3 years old
November 1991	Raymond Joseph Gosh	86 years old
September 1991	Steven "Rocky" Oerther	6 years old
April 1991	Nicholas A. Hinton	2 years old
April 1991	Ishmael Gonzales	8 years old
November 1990	Kayla Reaves	2 weeks old
October 1990	Jessica Cole	2 years old
August 1990	Richard Stitch, II	17 months old
July 18, 1990	Tionna Kenny	6 months old
July 1990	Jason Lee Wilson	5 years old
June 9, 1990	Betty Lou Stidham	57 years old
June 1990	Kelsey Provo	2 years old
March 1990	Laurene MacLeod	35 years old
February 27, 1990	Sarah Swineford	4 years old
January 1990	Ana Lynn Pagliaro	5 days old
December 1989	Alexander Jones	3 years old

Date of Death	Name	Age
November 1989	Garrett East	2 years old
October 20, 1989	Hoke Lane Prevette	20 years old
July 1989	Nelson Bunting	73 years old
May 1989	Dustin Webb	3 years old
March 1989	Angie Nickerson	5 years old
January 1989	April Loveless	4 years old
December 12, 1988	Amber Haverstock	6 months old
November 12, 1988	Douglas Semaken	5 years old
October 1988	Doyce Fielder, III	7 years old
September 1988	Nathan Carpenter	4 years old
September 3, 1988	Cara Rognaldsen	35 days old
May 1988	Melissa Boyse	16 months old
March 1988	Chatt (Chett) Hyder	2 years old
January 20, 1988	Megan Stack	2 years old
December 4, 1987	Brian Lillis	2 weeks old
September 24, 1987	Shannon Tucker	2 years old
July 4, 1987	Robert Barbarita	29 years old
June 13, 1987	James Soto	2.5 years old
April 6, 1987	Melissa Larabee	16 months old
April 6, 1987	William Eckman	67 years old
December 1986	Rachel Ann Blevins	3 years old
November 21, 1986	Billy Gordon, Jr.	4 years old
October 26, 1986	Fernando Salazar	3 years old
September 1986	Sarah Faye DeMos	2 years old
September 1986	Thomas Ebersole	7 years old
June 10, 1986	Kyle Corullo	20 months old
April 9, 1986	Christopher Dickey	5 years old
April 1986	Renee Smith	8 years old
February 2, 1986	Stephen Mark Fiengo, Jr.	6 years old
October 1985	Jessica Sue Huhn	4 years old
June 27, 1985	Melissa O'Rourke	3 years old
March 1985	Eckhardt Borchardt	6 years old
March 1985	James Shirley	2 years old
December 19, 1984	Gertrude Monroe	87 years old
December 11, 1984	Daniel Lloyd Smith	infant
October 14, 1984	Coral Robinson	2 months old
September 1984	Douglas E. Waddell, Jr.	2 years old
July 1984	Daniel Briggs	unknown
April 1984	Jacob Hoffer	6 years old

Date of Death	Name	Age
March 3, 1984	Rachel Hernandez	4 years old
February 1984	James Miller	4 years old
October 1983	Stephen Stanley	3 years old
October 22, 1983	Grace Parsons	67 years old
October 1983	Patricia Aliprandi	2 years old
July 7, 1983	Sara Lynn Delance	5 years old
July 1983	Jennifer Rasper	7 years old
June 1983	Marcellus Hampton	11 years old
April 1983	Baby "Doe"	1 week old
February 1983	Toby Daniel Brown	3 years old
October 17, 1982	Crystal Rose White	2 months old
September 1982	Paul Zechman	5 years old
June 1982	Roy Hamilton, Jr.	7 weeks old
May 1982	Angela Jones	7 years old
April 1982	Kerry Wezensky	5 years old
December 8, 1981	Daniel Thornton	infant
October 25, 1981	Ronald Messer	4 years old
August 1981	Jason Cabe	5 years old
April 1981	Kelly Brown	2 years old
exact date unknown 1981	Mary Logan	81 years old
exact date unknown 1981	"John Doe"	6 years old
December 29, 1980	Kevin Zook	14 years old
November 1980	Charles Vance Coleman	11 years old
April 27, 1980	Tonia Chester	3 years old
April, 1980	Nicole Klingenbeck	4 weeks old
February, 1980	Shannon Marie Hicok	27 days old
February 10, 1980	James Gradecki	1 month old
February 1980	Norman Ben, Jr.	3 years old
January 4, 1980	William Travis Crews	2 years old
October 30, 1979	Christopher Johnson	2 weeks old
December 1978	Jennifer Schafner	3 years old
September 1978	Danielle Nicole Russell	3 weeks old
December 1977	Jon Setzer, Jr.	3 years old
September 1977	Robert Boyd	7 months old
July 1977	Jeremy Tomkinson	3 months old
May 17, 1977	Mathew Cochran	6 months old
April 1977	Matthew Weck	5 years old
April 1977	Tamara Rhae Newton	6 years old
January 3, 1977	Darrell Enneking	6 years old

Date of Death	Name	Age
December 1976	Josh Gatlin	4 years old
September 1976	Carra Bashold	5 days old
August 1976	Christopher Simpson	4 years old
June 1976	Vincent Buffoleno	14 days old
May 15, 1976	Misty Lee	6 years old
August 1975	Michael Yount	5 years old
June 1975	Heidi Foust	3 years old
May 1975	Johnny Patterson, Jr.	2 years old
March 1975	Fern Atchley	75 years old
January 1975	Tracy Wax	5 months old
November 1974	Brent Cryder	5 years old
June 1974	Walter Schell	70 years old
May 14, 1974	Toni Lynn Edgeworth	5 years old
April 24, 1974	Lawrence Calemmo	6 years old
January 1974	David Scott Little	3 years old
August 14, 1972	Abel Valdivia	2 years old
March 5, 1972	Dawn Quintal	8 years old
September 19, 1971	Heidi Sufficool	21 months old
March 3, 1971	Karrie Fritz	3 years old
March 6, 1969	Susan Babiarz	1 month old
December 23, 1967	Darla Anne Harper	4 years old
December 17, 1967	Kenneth Goodman	4 years old
December 17, 1967	Gene Anthony Goodman	5 years old
August 3, 1966	Sharon K. Sparks	5 years old
June 8, 1966	Johnny Sunshine	3 years old
November 1965	Louis Rasmussen	60 years old
April 23, 1965	Marla Perry	4 years old
March 17, 1965	Vincent Scardina	22 months old
November 18, 1963	James Henderson	4 months old
October 23, 1963	Shari Nicoletti	2 years old
March 19, 1960	Frances Tetreault	50 years old
May 23, 1959	Mark Draper	2.5 years old
April 5, 1959	"Jane Doe"	58 years old
March 24, 1959	Billy Stillions	5 years old
November 24, 1958	Michael Kaminski	3 years old
August 11, 1955	Danny Betz	21 months old
March 1950	Donald A. Boucher	5 years old
January 1, 1948	infant May	1 month old

Date of Death	Name	Age
February 7, 1947	Walter Momer, Jr.	4 years old
January 31, 1947	Glen Howard Brace	5 years old
May 16, 1945	Doretta Zinke	39 years old
February 13, 1945	Marguerite Derdenger	21 months old
July 1943	May Jane Lund	2 years old
August 27, 1942	Dorothy Whipka	21 years old
February 9, 1942	Mrs. Albert McBain	60 years old
May 14, 1939	Raymond Gene Smith	4 years old
August 31, 1937	Charlotte Parker	65 years old
July 4, 1937	Maxwell Breeze	14 years old
March 21, 1934	Eunice Dean	4 years old
September 9, 1912	Mary Pisdarek	7 years old
March 29, 1912	Anna de Calve	3 years old
February 10, 1904	William Huston	57 years old
March 17, 1901	Carrie Cobus	38 years old
September 30, 1896	unnamed infant	unknown
September 30, 1896	Laura Barmann	7 years old
September 7, 1891	Edward Gillis	9 years old
January 30, 1887	Jane McElhenney	39 years old

Contents

For all your days be prepared, and meet them ever alike. When you are the anvil, bear; when you are the hammer, strike.

~Edwin Markham

Ham·mer

noun:
a tool with a heavy metal head mounted at right angles at the end of a handle, used for jobs such as breaking things and driving in nails

verb:
to hit or beat (something) with a hammer or similar object. "They are made by heating and hammering pieces of iron."

informal:
attack or criticize forcefully and relentlessly

Notes from the Author

The term, "The Hammer," is a figure of speech that I not only used for the title of this book, but also as a fitting description of the most powerful and devastating tool to occupy space in a wolf or dog's bag of survival equipment. That tool is aggression. When a person selects a hammer as their tool of choice, it is because they are confronting a task that requires brute force, not finesse, to beat an object into submission.

Use of the "Hammer" by dogs is real, and men, women, and children are subjected to its devastating effects in this country on a daily basis. Since 2005, over 400 Americans have been killed by dogs, and each year, nearly 4.5 million suffer from bites that require emergency room visits.[1] In 2015, more than 28,000 people underwent reconstructive surgery as a result of being bitten by dogs.[2] In the last decade, homeowner insurance claims for dog bites have risen 5.5% per year and now account for one third of all claims, costing Americans an average of $570 million dollars annually.[3] Successful criminal prosecution of dangerous dog owners has risen 62% in the past five years, while successful civil prosecution has risen 87%.[4] In a weak effort to lessen the number and severity of dog attacks, over 12 states and 700 cities in the U.S. and over 40 countries worldwide have enacted breed-specific legislation that bans or severely restricts breeds such as Pit Bulls and Rottweilers.[5] In an era of global education capabilities, and government and independent studies that continually cite evidence of a 5-7% increase in dog attacks annually, there is no excuse for such a high number of injuries and deaths. Yet they continue to happen, and if history repeats itself, which is almost certain, an even greater number of Americans will suffer death and severe injuries from dog attacks in the coming years.

Why will history repeat itself? One reason is that dog aggression as a whole is nothing more than an irritating smear on an otherwise seductive and bountiful landscape that has produced a 63-billion-dollar annual love affair between Americans and their pets. Although reports of dog attacks that result in serious injuries or fatalities are posted on the internet and broadcast over television when they first occur, they generally have no sustaining power due to the lack of support from the pet industry and the majority of the American dog-owning populous, which accounts for 65% of the households in the U.S.[6] A story of a dog attack typically hangs around just long enough to earn a few comments by medical and law enforcement personnel, a few frowns from the TV hosts, or a few empty promises to look into the problem by local officials, then it's swept under the rug and replaced with more current and mainstream news.

Americans love their dogs and don't want to hear anything negatively associated with them, especially something as terrible as an attack that ends in a fatality. It's like hearing about a shark attack at your favorite summertime beach resort. At first, the news is shocking, and then it saddens you because you really love that particular beach. Next, an expert on shark behavior is interviewed by local media outlets, and he or she assures the public that sharks don't like to eat people and the attack was most likely a chance encounter or a case of the shark mistaking the victim for natural prey. No fault is assigned to the shark, or the behavior of the victim, and the interview wraps up with an expert presenting an astronomical number that you quickly apply to the chances of such an attack happening to you instead of the thousands of other beach goers. After doing the math, you conclude that your favorite beach resort has always been and still remains perfectly safe to visit.

Harboring such an attitude of willful ignorance when it comes to the possibility that "man's best friend" could seriously harm you or even kill you has caused many victims to make fatal mistakes when they have encountered dangerous dogs. Because of their intentional blindness, they never saw the attack coming. The prominent expression captured on their faces after the attack was disbelief, especially when the attack came from a dog they had owned, loved, and cared for for many years. While interviewing survivors of serious, personally-owned dog attacks, I never was told that they knew such an attack was possible. On the contrary, a few of them believed they could suffer from an attack by a strange dog, albeit with a very remote chance, but never by their own dog. For them, such an act by their dog simply wasn't possible. Why did they foster this belief? Partly because they were human, and humans desperately hold to the notion that "if I love you, you will love me." If I take care of you, you will take care of me. If I do not harm you, you will not harm me. This way of thinking is a very romantic notion, but it is a human emotion nevertheless, and not one held by wolves or dogs. A dog will attack a human regardless of any amount of benevolence or love provided by that human if the dog ever perceives that human as a threat or an opponent in its acquisition of high-value food or objects, defense of its territory, or if it feels its life is in jeopardy. For most dog owners, this is a hard pill to swallow, but it is a real danger, and is highlighted in the four stories of fatal dog bite attacks that I write about.

The other part of the blame for the continuing rise in dog attacks, whether they occur from personal dogs or not, lies with a lack of proper education in regard to the cause of canine aggression and how to avoid it. The vast majority of information on the subject, doled out by various authors and professionals in the fields of dog behavior and healthcare, is distressingly inaccurate, too incomprehensible, or too broad in its scope for the average dog owner to utilize effectively. These professionals attempt to explain their reasons for aggression at the academia level, and attach them to a long list of causes that include lack of socialization, dominance, resource guarding, differing training methodologies, inhumane treatment by primary caregivers, and puppy mill production, just to name a few. To further the detriment of dog owner safety, other authors and professionals have even added to the list human-specific behaviors such as revenge, jealousy, and greed. And if having to sort through and understand all of their explanations of aggression wasn't enough, dog owners are additionally confronted with an overwhelming list of do's and don'ts that must be accurately paired with the right cause to successfully prevent their dog from attacking them or a non-family member. When dog attacks occur, they happen within seconds. Escape from harm requires a lightning-fast assessment of the type of aggression you are dealing with and the immediate implementation of the correct action(s) on your part to avoid it. The current overload of misguided information, coupled with faulty recommendations, has left most dog owners woefully confused and unprepared to effectively prevent and avoid an attack.

The message conveyed in this book was born from an urgent need to educate dog owners about the real causes of dog aggression, and what they must do when confronted with such aggression in order to avoid serious bodily harm or death. I have done my best to deliver this message as simply and directly as possible without straying from its intended path. Therefore, I did not overly elaborate on subject matter such as the when's and where's of the domestication process that propelled dogs from their former existence in the wild to their current existence in 79 million American households. I also did not entertain any arguments that imply that because the domestic dog has lived under man's influence for so long, it no longer shares any behavioral traits associated with the gray wolf. There is more than enough morphological, behavioral, and molecular evidence, not to mention my 50 years of personal observation and interaction with dogs, wolves, and other social predators, to strongly contest this erroneous belief.

I have also excluded puppies from this book because of the seriousness of the subject matter, and instead focused more on mature, adult dogs. Granted, a puppy can bite you, but it's extremely doubtful that the bite you receive from one will kill you or cause you to spend a lengthy stay in a hospital. Furthermore, I did not address dog-to-dog aggression because a dog will attack another dog for all of the same reasons it would attack a human. Therefore, I chose to stay away from any redundancy by selecting human safety over dog safety.

Lastly, I did not weigh in on the uncontrollable debate where narrow-minded combatants quarrel over their unswerving belief that certain breeds, such as Pit Bulls and Rottweilers, are all safe or are all deadly. My doing so would have only served as a meaningless distractor from the book's message. After all, you don't have to be an expert on canine aggression to realize that any breed of dog can attack you, but only a handful can kill you, and some do it more often than others. Instead, the message will be presented without any bias to any particular breed.

The stories presented in this book are based upon real events. The victims were not mere statistics, but real people with real lives. However, some names and events have been changed to preserve the privacy of the victims and their families. My intent in writing the stories was to bring a harsh reality to the actual causes of dog bite fatalities and to dispel the explanations that have continued to mislead humans and place them in harm's way for years.

I hope this book stirs our dog-loving society from the dream-like state that has enveloped us and convinced us that reports of dog attacks are sensationalized and exaggerated by the media and that the attacks that kill or injure people are only caused by deranged dogs suffering under the control of abusive owners. That's not the truth, and American dog owners need to be told the truth about dog aggression. They do not need to continue to be led down a deceptive road that proclaims "all will be well" as long as they provide enough love and socialization for their dogs. Wake up, America. Half of the 400 victims of dog attacks were killed by either their own dog, a family member's dog, or a friend's dog, and all of the dogs involved were well cared for and loved by the victims right up until the moment the attack occurred.

The "Hammer" is real, and the fact that with each passing year you could become a victim of it is real. Dogs do not need to be feared; rather, they need to be understood, and the behavior of humans that interact with dogs needs to change in accordance with this understanding. In this book, I have done my best to explain why dogs attack us, and I have explained how to prevent them from doing so. My hope is that someday, no man, woman, or child will ever die from the very real cause of canine aggression.

Earl May

The soft whisper of gravel under Earl May's feet carried a tune that reminded him of the lyrics from an old B.B. King song titled, "The Thrill is Gone." It was one of Earl's favorite songs, and he couldn't help but grin as he shuffled his worn leather shoes to keep time with B.B. King's raspy voice belting out how lonely he would be without his baby. *So lonely I'll be, too,* thought Earl, *if I don't hurry up and get home to my baby real soon!* Chuckling at the thought of the playful scolding he was sure to get from Mrs. May for staying out too late at his cousin Tommy's house and for partaking in a little (well, maybe more than a little) blackberry moonshine. Earl picked up the tempo until the gravel under his shoes sang a fair rendition of another B.B. King favorite, "Let the good times roll."

Earl was in an unusually good mood. Without a doubt, the clear, fiery liquid that had trickled down his throat all evening and the constant stream of southern-born jazz from Tommy's boom box had contributed to his mood, but, nevertheless, he was feeling quite content at the moment. Not even the arthritis that usually plagued his hands or the cataracts that severely limited his 79-year-old vision could keep him from snapping his fingers under a full October moon as he danced along the two-mile stretch of road that connected his house with Tommy's. Earl couldn't put a finger on his reason for feeling so content; he just was, and that was a feeling that hadn't visited him often in his life as a poor black man trying to make a living in rural Mississippi. With a little over a mile left to go before he was at the mercy of Mrs. May, Earl smiled and continued his snap, shuffle, and singing routine in front of an audience of cotton stalks, whose white, fibrous heads under the moonlight convinced Earl that the entire audience of cotton was smiling back.

At roughly the same time that Earl May was contentedly serenading the moonlit cotton stalks, Jeremiah Banks was getting ready to kill both of his dogs if he could ever get his hands on them. It was about an hour short of midnight when he discovered that his two 75-pound, male Pit Bulls were missing from his fenced yard. "Damn dogs," grumbled Jeremiah as he gazed down the beam of his flashlight at the spot in the fence where Boss and Pete had made their escape. Ralph, an old friend and local hardware store employee, had warned Jeremiah about using chicken wire to contain his dogs. "That wire ain't strong 'nuf to hold in dem mean dogs of yours, Jeremiah," Ralph had warned. "Dem dogs gonna git out and kill sumbody sum day!" Then he had pointed at another bale of wire and explained, "You gonna need that eleven-gauge cattle wire over there if you stand a snowball's chance in hell of keepin' dem dogs in yo yard!" Now, staring at the mangled and torn chicken wire, Jeremiah was wishing that he'd listened to Ralph and sprung for the material that was made to hold in cattle, instead of "cheapen' out on that no-good chicken wire." The last time they had gotten out, Boss and Pete had traveled over ten miles to a white man's farm and killed one of his calves. That incident had cost Jeremiah six hundred dollars; if you counted the day of work he'd missed having to apologize to a county judge for his dogs. He could still remember the tongue lashing he'd received from the judge and the stern warning that if his dogs got out and caused trouble again, the county would take them from him and put them down. "BOSS! PETE!" hollered Jeremiah. "Ya'll better get back here in dis damn yard if you wanna see daylight ever again! You hear me, boys? BOSS! PETE!" Jeremiah listened for any sign of his dogs returning while he cast his flashlight beam into the thick woods behind his house, over the cotton fields adjacent to each side, and down the gravel road that led to his neighbor Tommy and, unknowingly, to Earl May, whose shuffling gait was bringing him closer to Jeremiah's house and the two missing Pit Bulls with every strum of B.B. King's guitar. "Damn dogs. Better cause no trouble whilst you out there if you know what's good for you!" mumbled Jeremiah as he turned and headed back to the house.

"I'm too damn old to go lookin' for dem no-good rotten dogs in da middle of da damn night."

Jeremiah had just reached his front door when a piercing scream slammed into his consciousness. With one fist clinging to the rusty doorknob, he turned his head and his flashlight in the direction of the scream. "What wuz dat?" Jeremiah whispered as he stared into the darkness, his brain scrambling to identify the sound. "Boss? Pete? Wuz dat you?" Deep inside, where Jeremiah could feel his heart thumping wildly, he knew it wasn't. "No dog I know makes dat kinda sound, no sir, no dog. Dat was no animal." With that revelation, the chilly October air suddenly warmed, and Jeremiah felt sweat beading on his forehead. His breathing became short, desperate gasps. Gripping the doorknob even tighter, as though to ensure his escape, Jeremiah willed the flashlight to send its light over the edge of the cotton fields and along the row of pine trees, standing like dark, solemn guardians of his few remaining acres, until it stopped on its own. Jeremiah squinted down the length of the beam, but it wasn't necessary. Even from that distance, he knew what the beam had revealed, and a dread as deep as a man would ever want to know slowly set in. At the furthest edge of the light were fresh tracks, left in a small depression that was still muddy from the previous night's rain. They belonged to his Pit Bulls, Boss and Pete, and their path was headed towards Tommy's house - the same direction from which he had heard the horrifying scream a moment ago. "No, no, sweet Jesus, no, please," whispered Jeremiah as he closed his eyes for a few seconds and muttered a prayer that the light would reveal his eyes had been mistaken and that all would be ok. With his hands trembling, he slowly opened his eyes and raised the flashlight beam until it reached the furthest end of the tracks and was swallowed by a deep and forbidding blackness. For several minutes, Jeremiah gazed solemnly at the dark, like he had done so many times in his life, then switched off the flashlight and slumped against the door. It wasn't the first time Jesus had said no to Jeremiah.

"You say Earl left over two hours ago after he'd been drinking that moonshine of yours all evening?" Mrs. May's initial agitation toward her husband was quickly becoming one of concern as she listened to Tommy's slurred confession over the phone.

"And you just let him walk home like that and didn't call me first?" Mrs. May snapped, the question more of a condemnation than an inquiry.

"He dun it befo' and you ain't thought nothin of it then!" rebutted Earl's cousin.

"Tommy, it's a good thing you're on the other end of this phone, or I'd snatch what little hair you have left off that stupid head of yours!" cried Mrs. May as she slammed the phone back on its cradle. "Where could that old man possibly be?" she wondered out loud as she leaned on the walker that had become a necessary part of her movement after she had fallen and broken her hip a few months back. Staring in disbelief at the large hands on the clock that had found a permanent place on the wall just above the TV opposite of Earl's favorite easy chair, she muttered, "It's midnight! He's never taken two hours to walk home from Tommy's, moonshine or no moonshine." Something was terribly wrong, but in an effort to stave off the panic that was threatening to claim what composure she had left, Mrs. May began to search her mind for a possible explanation as she hobbled to the front door to peek outside for the tenth time that night. Her thoughts were racing: maybe he had stopped to smoke that God-awful pipe of his, like he'd done a few other times? Heaven forbid, he knows I won't let him smoke that thing here! Despite her growing anxiety, she almost chuckled at the thought of Earl trying to fill the pipe's bowl with tobacco while walking, after he'd already helped himself to Tommy's moonshine. Like Hansel and Gretel, he'd have left a trail all the way back to Tommy's, except it would have been that nasty-smelling cheap tobacco instead of bread crumbs! Yes, that had to be it, and to affirm her answer, Mrs. May turned to the small table next to the door where Earl kept his pipe. Being careful not to pull too hard on the twice-fixed broken handle on the table's only drawer, Mrs. May slowly opened the drawer and searched its contents. At first, she didn't see the pipe. Its shape was blocked by several forbidden tins of snuff, which enabled Earl to secretly enjoy his tobacco inside the house. "At least so he thinks," smiled Mrs. May. Even though she hated it, she had always pretended not to notice. She loved Earl too much to keep him from all of his vices. However, after she got her hands on him tonight, she was going to curtail the vice called moonshine for a spell. It was only after she pulled the tins of snuff out of the drawer that she noticed the pipe and a small bag of tobacco in the back. Her heart sank immediately, and the panic that had momentarily abated returned with more conviction than before. "Where is my Earl? There has to be an explanation as to why he's taking so long to come home. If he didn't stop to smoke his pipe, then there has to be another reason." Turning back to the front door, Mrs. May peeked outside again to see if she could make out Earl's swaggering form coming down the gravel road that would have taken him past Jeremiah's place and put him on his way home from Tommy's. "That's it! Earl must have stopped by Jeremiah's house, where he's most likely separating Mr. Banks from his moonshine, too! I just hope Jeremiah had enough sense to put those two dogs of his up first. Can't understand why he keeps them dogs. Mean as the devil, they are." With that, Mrs. May gripped her walker and shuffled to the phone on the wall to call Jeremiah. "I know it's too late to be calling, but surely he's up and trading stories with Earl. Heck, between him and Earl, there are enough stories to fill up the library in this town twice! Let the moonshine start flowing, and the two of them will make up enough other stories to justify building a third library all together!"

"Hello?" On the sixth ring, Jeremiah's sister Ellen answered.

"Ms. Ellen, this is Earl's wife. I am so sorry to be calling you so late, but I was wondering if Earl was there, and if he is, would you tell him I said to get home right this minute?" Mrs. May held her breath as she waited for Ellen to tell her that her Earl was indeed there.

"Don't be sorry for calling so late, girl, but Earl ain't here. Neither is Jeremiah for dat matter," answered Ellen.

"Oh. Did Earl and Jeremiah go off somewhere?" Mrs. May still held her breath.

"No ma'am. I ain't seen your Earl. Jeremiah's gone lookin' for dem dogs of his. They dun got outta da yard again and took off up da road towards Tommy's house. Maybe Jeremiah won't find dem dis time. Maybe they'll git killed by a car or somethin' befo' they kill somethin' else! If Tommy finds dem, he'll shoot dem for sure! He's like me and don't like dem dogs, and he dun told Jeremiah befo' he'd shoot 'em if he ever caught dem in his yard!" Like Tommy and Mrs. May, Ellen had always feared for her safety with Jeremiah's dogs around, but because it was his house and he had always allowed her to stay there between jobs, drug addictions, and marriages, she had always been careful about expressing her feelings about the dogs. On the one occasion when she had, Jeremiah had become extremely defensive. "Dem dogs ain't gonna hurt you. You do a fine 'nuff job of dat on your own! I keeps dem dogs so nobody takes what lil' stuff I have. You should appreciate dat!" Ellen was certain that if it came down to her or the dogs staying with Jeremiah, she'd be headed down the same gravel road those damn dogs had headed down tonight! It was while she was contemplating this that she noticed the silence on the other end of the phone. "Mrs. May, you there? Hello? Mrs. May?"

Mrs. May didn't hear Ellen calling for her. All of her attention had turned to a painting of Jesus praying in the garden of Gethsemane hanging on the wall by the small oval kitchen table where she and Earl had eaten, prayed, and made all of their major decisions in their fifty years of marriage. The painting had faded from the sunlight that bathed it most mornings, and the frame was cracked in a few places from all the times it had fallen off the wall due to Earl's lack of handyman skills.

With a sickening feeling in her heart, Mrs. May loosened her grip on her walker and slowly lowered her weary frame to the floor, where she took up the same position as Jesus in the painting, as she had done so many times in her life. Bringing her trembling hands to her mouth, Mrs. May closed her eyes and whispered Earl's name over and over, begging him to come home. She waited to hear his dancing shuffle on the gravel road or the creak of the front door opening, followed by a string of Earl's imaginative excuses for drinking and staying out too late, but none came. Only the tick-tock of a distant clock and the beat of her heart made their presence known. Still on her knees, Mrs. May turned and looked at the clock for the hundredth time that night and suddenly became aware of a brilliant harvest moon framed by her kitchen window. "Oh, Earl. Please remember your promise," Mrs. May tearfully plead to the moon. "Please don't leave me alone." And then, for the second time that night, a prayer was sent from a home on a rural gravel road in Mississippi, and for a second time, Jesus said no.

Earl May had snapped and shuffled his way through all of the B.B. King songs he thought he knew when the exhaustion from his ambitious performance and an evening of sipping moonshine turned into a well-deserved smoke break. Shuffling to the side of the gravel road, Earl made his way to a familiar tree stump that, like nearly everything in those parts, had become almost invisible by the very relentless kudzu growing on it. Using one hand to guide his butt to the stump, Earl used his other to fish in his coat pocket for the briar wood pipe and the half empty pouch of 4 Aces Silver tobacco that he had put in there before he'd left his house. "Well, I'll be damned," muttered Earl when his fishing came up empty. "What'd I do with dat pipe?" Earl fished in his other coat pocket, and when that came up empty, too, he leaned back on the stump to check his front pockets for what he was certain would be the location of his instrument of pleasure. Earl's hands hadn't quite made contact with his trousers when the moonshine buzz took over and sent him tumbling off the back of the stump, where he landed on his back staring up at a huge orange circle that seemed to fill the entire night sky. Oh how Mrs. May loved a harvest moon like the one that was glistening above him at that moment. Every fall, she would always take his hand and make him promise to the rising orange sphere that they would always be together. "I promise," whispered Earl confidently while still lying on his back and staring up at the moon. In all their years of marriage, and through one setback after another, it was the one thing he had never failed to do. With fifty harvest moons as his witness, Earl had always kept his promise to his girl.

"Sorry old man, I gotta git home, or there might not be nuthin' to promise come next year." Earl winked at the moon and, with a bit more effort than it should have taken, managed to pull himself back up to the stump. Catching his breath before attempting the next stage of actually standing, Earl took in the beauty of the cotton fields and the pines as they bathed in the glow of the moon. "Can't find this in no city. No sir, you can't. Only thing mo' pretty is dat girl of mine." Earl flashed the biggest smile he'd flashed all evening as he pulled himself up and gingerly made his way through the maze of kudzu to the gravel road. It was when he turned in the direction that would take him to his girl that he noticed the gravel road seemed to move on its own at the furthest end of the moon's rays ahead of him. "Whoa, I ain't gonna drink no mo' of dat liquor of Tommy's," chuckled Earl as he wiped his eyes with the sleeve of his shirt. "Unless my dancin' dun caused da road to wanna dance with me, and if dat's da case, Ms. Road, I hope you can keep up!" Laughing out loud, Earl looked down at the road and did his best to cut his famous Earl the Emancipator groove on an old tire rut. Earl had earned the nickname from his friends, who said his willingness to dance anytime, anywhere, and to any song was so inspiring that it freed others from the bondage of sitting still.

Unbeknownst to Earl, the movement he had mistaken for an imaginary dancing partner was the very real forms of Boss and Pete racing full speed toward him. With keen senses designed for nocturnal hunting, Boss and Pete had detected Earl's presence several hundred yards back, and like the farmer's calf they had slaughtered and much of the prey killed by wolves, Earl was a chance encounter; an encounter that would serve to temporarily fulfill a primitive but un-repealed need thousands of years old: the need to kill.

Earl the Emancipator was making good work of the tire rut and was teaching the road a thing or two about dancing when he heard his name called. Stopping halfway through a spin, he tried to focus on both his balance and whether he had actually heard his name or just imagined it. "Mrs. May?" Earl questioned as he searched for the voice. Through blurred vision, his gaze followed the moon's rays to the spot where the road had appeared to be moving a few seconds ago before his dance lesson. To his surprise, the road was still moving, but the movement had transformed into an unrecognizable shape rapidly approaching him. "Mrs. May, is dat you?" It had to be her thought Earl. After all, it was a woman's voice he'd heard, and who else would be headed down that road at that time of the night calling his name? Earl couldn't help but shake his head at the thought of Mrs. May coming after him, walker and all, acting upset and fussing about his drinking. "Hell, I bet she dun cut one of dem switches she used to get after our boy with, and now she's 'bout to get after me!" Laughing at the thought, Earl staggered backwards with his hands up and shouted a feigned "I give" toward the shape that was sure to be Mrs. May coming to fetch him home.

Earl was still laughing and staggering backwards when the shape suddenly and unexpectedly took on the form of a low-moving black mass that resembled nothing like Mrs. May. Earl stopped dead in his tracks and lowered his arms. "What da hell?" he hissed as he watched the mass suddenly split and become two masses. Earl's mind was having a difficult time comprehending what he had just witnessed. A hard life had borne more incomprehensible events than Earl cared to remember, but nothing like the one playing out in front of him at the moment. Danger screamed at Earl from the deepest recesses of his mind and shook him to his core in an attempt to propel him into action. However, another part of his mind, the part that had always tried to make sense of an incomprehensible world, and the one most affected by the moonshine, refused to cooperate. Acting as perfect opponents, the two parts of his mind defeated one another and left Earl too confused and too drunk to move. As he continued to watch the forms racing toward him, Earl could feel the gravel road shake beneath his feet, and he heard what sounded like thunder at a distance. As the two forms closed the distance to within a few feet, the thunder escalated into a deafening roar. With unbelievable speed, the two Pit Bulls hurled themselves toward Earl, who stood transfixed as though he were in a terrible, terrible dream. But it wasn't in a dream that Earl recognized the forms that were bearing down on him. It was those killer dogs belonging to Jeremiah, and death had come with them. "Oh, sweet Jesus..." whimpered Earl. Like any other man, Earl knew he would die one day, but he had always assured himself that he would be ready when the time came because he was a man of faith, and Jesus had promised he would live on streets of gold where there was no pain, no fear, and no more sadness for those who believed. But at that moment, Earl could only think of his girl of fifty years and how the voice he'd heard had to have been a warning from her. For a fraction of a second, Earl started to smile. To the very end, Mrs. May was always trying to look after him. But as soon as the smile started, it ended, as Earl thought of what his death would do to the woman he loved so very much. He became terribly afraid and terribly sad. In the last second before impact, Earl glanced at the moon and pleaded for it to tell his wife that he was sorry he had broken his promise.

The Four Factors of An Attack

A few years ago, I was helping a new client train her puppy, when she felt the need to remove her jacket because the morning's chill had worn off. Handing me the leash to her puppy, she pulled off her jacket and laid it on the ground next to her backpack. When she straightened and reached towards me to retake the leash, the t-shirt she had been wearing underneath exposed a horribly disfigured right arm with jagged, pink and white scars covering its entire length. The shock on my face must have been obvious, because before I could recover and resume my teachings on puppy imprinting, she muttered, "My cousin's dog attacked me for no reason." Having spent the previous three decades studying and working with social predators, and witnessing the destruction their jaws and claws had done to muscle and bone many times, I thought I had grown somewhat immune to its effect; obviously, I hadn't. Perhaps I was caught off guard because the damaged muscle and bone belonged to a beautiful girl and the grotesque scars contradicted her beauty, or perhaps it was because I had detected a familiar cry of disbelief in her remark.

Either way, I was deeply moved, and it was all I could do to be heard when I asked her why the dog attacked her. "I'm not sure why", she answered. "One minute I was petting it like I had done a million times before, and the next minute, it was trying to tear my arm off!" She became silent as she stared at her arm and into an ugly past. Then, suddenly, she bent over, picked up her jacket and put it back on. The morning chill had returned.

I have interviewed thousands of dog bite victims and I have researched the facts surrounding hundreds of dog attack fatalities. In each case, immediately after the attack, emotions ran high and reasoning ran low, and words such as "unprovoked" and "motiveless" were attached to the attacking dog's actions by the surviving victims and the families of the deceased. Outsiders, not having a personal stake in the incident, were not so quick to blame the dog, and attached words like "abuse" and "careless" to the actions of the victims. When both sides lobbied the opinions of experts in canine behavior to support their reasons for the attack, they often received ineffective rulings that were supported more by public sentiment than by actual science. All of this contributed greatly to chaos, but it did nothing in the way of teaching us why dogs attack us and how to prevent them from doing so. Therefore, I focused my attention on the facts surrounding each case, and did not allow myself to get caught up in the chaos. I did this in hope that a common denominator would reveal itself; some sort of action or state of mind that acted in the way of a catalyst for all of the attacks. I knew if I found it, it would have to be the starting point from which any achievable plan for preventing canine aggression would grow.

After years of sifting through the rubble left by the decimated lives of dog attacks, I uncovered the common denominator I was so desperately looking for. Sadly, it reared its head in the form of a terribly misguided mindset that allowed the victims to literally wander, unawares, straight into the jaws of their attackers. This was a very disturbing find because even though avoiding the attack was impossible in a small percentage of the cases I researched, such was the case with Earl May, it was relatively easy for most of the others. This is especially true when you take into consideration that all that is necessary to successfully avoid an attack is a rudimentary knowledge of canine behavior, the ability to accurately interpret the warning signals given by a dog when it intends to bite you, and the understanding to then implement a few corrective actions on your part. However, the victims did not possess a rudimentary knowledge of canine behavior. Like my client, they also did not recognize the warning signals being given by the dog that foretold an attack was about to occur, and they failed to take the correct actions to either avoid the attack or save themselves when the attack was underway. Instead, they became lost in the moment and were carried to an apocalyptic end by what I call "**The Four Factors of an Attack**" - disbelief, blindness, ignorance, and speed. Each one was created by the common misguided mindset I discovered, but unique and deadly in their combined ability to create confusion and calamity in the critical seconds leading up to a dog's aggressive response to its victim's behavior.

Disbelief

If eyes are truly mirrors of the soul, then disbelief resided in the hearts of all of the victims of dog attacks I have ever interviewed. With each glazed look and each tear that fell, proof that they never considered, even for a second, that they would be bitten by the dog they were interacting with at the time was given. The majority of the victims harbored such disbelief because the attacking dog had either belonged to them, a family member, or a very close friend, and they had presumed that the dog would naturally trust and accept them because of their familial relationship with it, and therefore never want to bite them. The other victims were not familiar with their attackers and yet, they too, did not believe they would be bitten by the dog they had encountered. The reason for their disbelief was because they had somehow been convinced a dog would have to be justifiably provoked through the use of physical abuse, or be sufficiently threatened, to ever bite someone. In other words, as long as they didn't do anything evil or abusive, they believed their interaction with any dog would go off without a hitch. Even so, many of the victims of both groups gave cause to their disbelief, and quite possibly their own tragedy, when, at some point, they fell for the negligent and distorted notion that dogs possess "human-like" qualities in regard to moral conduct, instead of the ones that attempted to shred them to pieces! Continuously brainwashed by volumes of erroneous information advocating that dogs have developed extraordinarily powerful cognitive-developmental mechanisms like humans, they came to believe that love and kindness was the answer to any bad dog behavior, including aggression. Acting out on their belief, these naive victims confronted the dog's snarls and growls with hugs and kisses, and then had to not only suffer the pain of their wounds, but the pain of making sense of morality turned on its head.

Blindness

Nearly all of the victims interviewed admitted to being **blind** to the warning signs that were communicated by the dog prior to its attack. Many of them had depended upon unmistakable visual and/or auditory signals, such as growling or showing of the teeth, to warn them of the possibility of a bite. Therefore, when such signals were not presented by the attacking dog, the victims unknowingly continued with behaviors that eventually got them bitten. They did not realize that signals foretelling of an imminent attack by a dog are sometimes extremely subtle, and are not always a great display of bodily and facial expressions. For example, when the torso of the dog they were petting suddenly became stiff and rigid, or when the dog began regarding them out of the corner of its eyes as they extended their hand towards it, the victims were being told by the dog to stop what they were doing and move away. However, because they did not know what either of those signals meant, the victims continued with what they were doing and eventually provoked the dog's aggression, instead of carrying out behaviors that would have de-escalated the situation and put a stop to the attack.

Ignorance

The victims' **ignorance** of what motivated the dog to bite them played a major role in nearly all of the attacks. When asked to look back on the event, most victims could not recall what the dog was doing prior to the attack, let alone explain why they thought the dog bit them. Their answers highlighted an extremely problematic condition in regard to preventing future attacks: it's one thing to not recognize the signals of an impending attack being communicated by a dog, but it's a whole other to not ever know why you were attacked in the first place! As if to prove this point, over 30% of those I interviewed volunteered the information that the same dog had bitten them more than once. I wasn't surprised by their admissions, because if you can't assign an accurate explanation for your first attack, then you are helpless to prevent a repeat attack by the same dog for possibly the same reason (or any other dog for any other reason). When it comes to interacting with dogs, ignorance is not bliss. You must know the reasons why a dog will attack you and avoid doing anything that will cause it to do so.

Speed

The fourth and final factor involved in all of the attacks was the **speed** in which the dog aggressively reacted to its victim. That speed, standard across the board, was unimaginably fast! In fact, the acceleration from which a peaceful encounter with the dog turned into one in which the victims found themselves in a fight for their lives was more shocking to most of them than the attack itself. One particular lady I interviewed declared she would never again own or trust a dog because she found it impossible to comprehend how quickly the dog she loved turned into a dog that nearly killed her. When I asked an older male victim how long it took for the mastiff he was petting to chomp off two of his fingers, he blinked and said, "twice that fast."

In the wild, for aggression to be effective, it has to be swift. Even the slow, suffocating constriction of a python is preceded by a lightning fast strike and bite to its victim. Domestic dogs, because of their wolf ancestry, find no exception to this rule. Their bite may come with varying levels of power and purpose, but it will always come with a speed most humans find nearly imperceptible and almost impossible to avoid. Therefore, even if the victims had been able to recognize that they were going to be attacked, they would have had to act very quickly and in the right way to avoid it.

An awareness of "The Four Factors of an Attack" is absolutely necessary for the safety of humans during all dog encounters. This is because any of the factors by themselves can easily influence and manipulate the human-to-dog encounter into becoming a disaster, but in most cases the factors don't work by themselves. Instead, they work as a sadistic and insidious team, in which one factor hands the "Hammer" to the next factor, who hands it to the next, and so forth, until all four have done their damage. For instance, fostering the <u>disbelief</u> that you will be bitten by a dog will leave you <u>blind</u> to any warning signs the dog may exhibit, which will make you <u>ignorant</u> of the manner in which you are engaging the dog, which could provoke the dog to attack you with a <u>speed</u> you will not be able to counter safely and effectively. This is exactly how it has played out for millions of dog bite victims and it will continue to do so for millions more unless we come to believe that any dog, regardless of its ownership, may attack us, and learn why it would do so. We will also have to become acquainted with the signals that dogs communicate when an attack is about to happen, and then quickly perform the correct actions on our part to stop the attack or lessen its affect. We have to do this, because "The Four Factors of an Attack" cannot be ignored or discounted as conjecture; for they are the very real creation of the typical human-to-dog mentality, and devastation and death often come with them.

The Hammer is Forged

As discussed in the previous chapter, our **ignorance** of why dogs bite us is one of the leading reasons why people behave in ways that get them attacked. Therefore, our understanding of why and how dogs employ the "Hammer" is vital to adjusting our behavior and preventing its use against us. However, because all dog behavior, including aggression, finds its origin in wolf behavior, we must first come to understand why the "Hammer" was forged and how it is utilized by wolves before we can begin to understand its use by dogs against humans. Even though dogs have undergone significant morphological and biological alterations through the domestication process, behavioral changes have been much less sublime. Consequently, endeavoring to explain the cause of dog aggression without first addressing the cause of wolf aggression is baseless in its attempt. In his book, *Societies of Wolves and Free-ranging Dogs*, author and scientist Stephen Spotte supports my claim that, at the molecular level, dogs are still wolves, and it is from this level that their behavior is anchored. Stephen writes, *"The insistence that behavior and biology are inseparable might seem frustrating to those who* *measure only behavior's visible aspects. However, mechanism underlies expression at every level, and behaviorists ignore this truth at their peril. So-called 'cognitive' studies are misnamed when the observer describes a result and ignores the cause. Observation alone offers limited explanatory power if its goal is understanding how and why animals behave as they do."*[7]

The "Hammer" was forged because wolves are social predators (hunt as a pack to capture prey) that exist under a condition known as the **law of limited resources**, where the demand for food is often greater than the supply. This condition causes a fierce and sometimes deadly competition with members of the same pack, rival wolf packs, and other predators, such as bears, mountain lions, and coyotes, for an often-minimal supply of food. With wolves, competition also extends to reproduction, with the breeding pair controlling mating within the pack. Therefore, for the successful continuance of wolves as a species, nature needed to create a versatile and dependable tool for wolves to use that was lethal enough to easily kill large prey, vanquish their rivals, eliminate their threats, and maintain their established territories. But, the tool's ferociousness had to be tempered enough to allow wolves to adjust the behavior of other pack members without injuring, or killing them. The "Hammer" became that tool and footprints of the six purposes for which it is used by wolves to sustain their existence can be found in all dog attacks to humans.

1. Killing Prey

At the most fundamental level, life for a predator is an exchange of energy for more energy. Because wolves are carnivores, energy comes from ingesting and digesting the flesh of other living animals. The wolf's need for aggression to obtain the energy-providing flesh lit the flames of the furnace thousands of years ago, from which the "Hammer" was forged. Even though wolves are also scavengers and opportunists that take advantage of occasional carcasses left by nature or other predators, the living rodents, birds, herbivores, and ungulates they hunt when not scavenging do not give up their lives willingly so wolves may survive. Wolves have to capture and kill them by utilizing deadly force. Many ethologists and behaviorists do not consider the use of such deadly force for food acquisition as "aggression;" instead, they label it as a "component" of feeding and subsistence behavior. However, I am quite certain that the opinion of any rodent, bird, herbivore, or ungulate being attacked by a wolf would differ greatly from that of these experts. After all, the wolf does not come in peace bearing documents of negotiable terms while pleading its role as a predator in the predator vs. prey evolutionary scheme. Instead, it comes with jaws and claws that are utilized with imperceptible speed and power to catch, kill, dissect, and ingest its prey. By using the "Hammer", the wolf obtains life-sustaining energy until it is necessary to repeat the process all over again.

2. Interspecific Control

While in the process of acquiring life-sustaining energy, wolves frequently find themselves in interspecific (not of the same species) competition for the same limited amount of prey. When interspecific conditions present themselves to wolves, they often use the "Hammer" against their competitors in an attempt to secure the food for themselves. Wolves have even been known to attack or harass very deadly competitors such as bears and cougars in an attempt to drive them away from the remains of a recent kill they had made. When the wolves are successful, they profit in not only obtaining a meal, but also by depriving the other competing predator of its hard-earned meal, which weakens that predator and compromises its ability to compete with wolves again in the future.

In other cases involving interspecific competition, wolves profit from the very direct result of eliminating their competition all together. Such was the case during the reintroduction of the gray wolves into the Greater Yellowstone National Park. From 1995 to 1996, thirty-one gray wolves from two separate Canadian packs were released into the park in an attempt to restore the natural balance of the ecosystem that had become extremely unbalanced when wolves were killed or driven from the region in the early 1930s. The first order of business for the newly arrived wolves was the elimination of the current apex predator, the coyote, whose numbers had risen to the highest levels ever recorded with the wolves missing. The coyotes, which were a direct competitor for prey that consisted of elk, pronghorns, and small mammals, became the wolves' target. In less than three years, the wolves' relentless pursuit of total domination resulted in a reduction of the coyote population by up to 90% in the crucial, prey-wielding areas of the park; thus, the reigning apex predator was usurped from its position.

3. Intraspecific Control

As the wolf pack slowly grows in numbers, the establishment of a linear hierarchy, which is a form of intraspecific (of the same species) control, serves as a natural regulator of the "Hammer's" use in settling disputes that arise over competition for food and mating authority. Because all members of the pack are powerful predators capable of inflicting great harm or even death to each other, the "Hammer" must strike more softly when it is used to control the behavior of individual pack members. Otherwise, the pack could weaken itself and jeopardize its survival with the onset of debilitating injuries that would handicap vital members from assisting in hunts or defending the territory. Softening of the "Hammer" strike is accomplished, by and large, through a series of established, predictable, and recognizable dominant and submissive behaviors communicated by individual members of the pack to one or more other members. The behaviors, which comprise visual, haptic, and auditory responses, are often very successful at lessening the "Hammer's" blow or deflecting it all together. The overall goal of the softening of the "Hammer's" strike is the adjustment of undesired behaviors within the pack without the use of excessive energy or physical force that can be crippling and counterproductive to the survival of the pack.

4. Territorial Defense

Territorial defense is another form of intraspecific control by wolves. However, the aggression it uses is far more lethal than what is used to control inner pack behavior, because it is applied to trespassing alien wolves that attempt to poach vital resources or threaten the safety of cubs. After staking exclusive claim to a parcel of land that is large enough to provide adequate opportunities for successful hunts and protection of the young, a wolf pack will fiercely defend it by running down and killing any alien wolves caught hunting within its boundaries. By doing so, direct competition by alien wolves is eliminated, and the limited resources contained within the boundaries of the established territory are left only for the possessing pack.

5. Reproduction Control & Protection

After acquiring and safeguarding life-sustaining energy, life for the wolf focuses on the continuance of its species through reproduction. Wolves are highly social predators that cooperatively hunt in packs for large prey such as elk, caribou, moose, and deer. The pack is usually created by the mating of an unrelated pair of dominant wolves that had previously dispersed from their individual packs. However, in heavily saturated wolf populations where disbursement by individual wolves is made extremely difficult by the lack of vacant territorial space needed to safely locate a mate and raise offspring, mating will occur with a dominant pair that is related. Regardless of their relationship, the two mating wolves are known as the alpha pair, and it is here that the "Hammer" is used by the pair to lay claim to one another and aggressively discourage any attempt by subordinate pack members to breed with their respective mate. The pair will also use the "Hammer" to prevent other inbreeding attempts within the pack. Such control is necessary because the feeding of additional cubs, beyond those of the alpha pair, is often impossible with their limited food supply. If the pack's territory is hemmed in by other established territories, adult wolves are not able to disperse and make room for the additional cubs by leaving the pack with fewer mouths to feed. The "Hammer" effectively limits reproduction within a pack to the best gene pool by only allowing the alpha pair to mate; in turn, this acts as a governor to ensure that the population is maintained at healthy and sustainable levels.

When wolf cubs are born, the "Hammer" is utilized by all members of the pack in a communal effort to safeguard their existence. The adult wolf is an apex predator and does not suffer from natural predation in the United States and Canada; however, wolf cubs do not share in that luxury and have to be vigorously defended by the adult wolves from predators such as golden eagles, bears, mountain lions, and alien wolves until they reach the age of approximately one year old. At that age, most surviving wolf cubs have matured enough to defend themselves from all but the most seasoned and powerful invading wolves.

6. Self-Defense

For an adult wolf, a threat often manifests itself in the form of an alien wolf, a bear, or mankind. As an option to the use of the "Hammer" during deadly encounters with such threats, nature gave wolves the ability of flight as a means of escape. However, the election of flight does not always prove to be successful. Sometimes a wolf is run down by a faster and more determined alien wolf. Sometimes a wolf is cornered with its back pressed up against a rock wall by a mother bear that has taken offense to the wolf sizing up her cubs. Sometimes an unlucky wolf finds its broken paw held firmly by a steel trap as a man approaches with the intent to kill it. When flight fails in the face of a threat, no matter the circumstance, the one guarantee is that the "Hammer" will swing. However, unlike the other uses of the "Hammer", the violent force of self-defense serves only the purpose of securing escape or neutralizing the threat. Once the ability of flight is obtained or the threat is neutralized, aggression ceases.

An endless need for competitive resourcefulness lit the flame that heated the iron from which the "Hammer" was forged. For thousands of years, nature's breath fanned the flames as a hostile and competitive eco-niche, working alongside her and pummeling the iron until both had erased any semblance of malleability from its design. This was necessary because any softness would have only served to weaken the "Hammer," which needed to be hard and without mercy in its application if wolves were to have the violent tool they desperately needed to stay alive in a kill-or-be-killed existence. In time, life was breathed into the iron and wolves soon mastered its many purposes, which they used to become one of the most successful predators of all time. This is important to know because wolves passed the mighty "Hammer" to our dogs, who use it for many of the same reasons to survive in an eco-niche where perceived threats and competitors come in the form of human beings.

Changes to the Hammer in Dogs

The utilization of the "Hammer" by today's dogs finds its roots in the same purposes for which it was intended to be used by wolves. However, the main difference lies in how the selective pressures of thousands of years of domestication and mankind's obsession with eliminating some wolf-like behaviors in dogs, while reinforcing others, has had an effect on each intended purpose and the aggression needed to accomplish it. For instance, the intended use of the "Hammer" by wolves for the purpose of killing prey follows a specific hunting sequence that consists of four steps that precede the actual kill, and two that follow after the kill if the hunt is successful. The steps are: 1. locate 2. stalk 3. chase 4. catch 5. kill (the "Hammer") 6. dissect 7. ingest. However, dogs like Rat Terriers and Dachshunds have morphed from wolves to canines that only perform steps 1-5 when killing vermin, while dogs like Border Collies only perform steps 1-3 while herding sheep. The undesirable steps of 6 and 7, and 4-7, respectively, were deliberately arrested through mankind's control of each breed's genetic engineering, and their natural behavioral traits, thereby radically altering their instinctual use of the "Hammer" as it relates to killing prey. Another, and even more radical, example of how time and man's influence have impacted the use of the "Hammer" in regard to killing prey is a breed of dog known as the Great Pyrenees. Instead of killing prey such as sheep to acquire life-sustaining energy, like its ancestor, the wolf, still does, the Great Pyrenees now protects the prey (sheep) from being killed by wolves, so that the sheep can feed humans, who in turn feed the Great Pyrenees. In all cases of killing prey, innate aggression used for the purpose of food acquisition by wolves, was scaled back, refitted, or redirected by mankind in a way that worked for the benefit of his survival more than that of the domestic dog's.

However, changes in the application of the "Hammer" by dogs in regard to <u>intraspecific control</u>, <u>territorial defense</u>, and <u>self-defense</u>, have been driven more by environmental influences than by the direct manipulation of humans who, in the beginning, were more concerned with modifying canine aggression for the purpose of hunting and protecting livestock than for taming a wild wolf so it could become a companion. As a result, the aggression needed by dogs to fulfill the purposes of intraspecific control, territorial defense, and self-defense has not suffered the same level of degradation or deflection as the aggression used for killing prey. Instead, it has simply evolved to accomplish the function of each in an eco-niche filled with *humans* living in houses and apartments, instead of with wolves and other competing predators living in the wild. In simpler terms, it's not the level of aggression that has changed with each application; it's the environment and who it's used against that has changed for dogs. This is extremely alarming, because dogs are not human and humans are not dogs, so neither species instinctually knows for sure how to behave with the other species. Therefore, both dogs and humans have a tendency to gravitate toward what comes natural to them, especially during stressful conditions. As a result, if a dog ever feels the need to use aggression to adjust the behavior of a human who is attempting to take something of value from it, or is trespassing on their perceived territory, or is posing as a threat, the dog is likelier to use a level of violence that is more intrinsically aligned with **inter**specific control (wolf to coyote) than **intra**specific control (wolf to wolf). This has made dog attacks to humans for these reasons more damaging because a wolf will not purposely injure or kill a member of its pack for attempting to steal a morsel of food, but it will eviscerate a trespassing or poaching coyote (different species) without hesitation for the same offense! Unlike the adjustment to the application of the "Hammer" for killing prey that has benefited mankind's survival, the adaptation that has occurred to intraspecific control, territorial defense and self-defense has only served to benefit dogs. With dog ownership in the U.S. growing at a steady rate of 3.5 million dogs per year, the attempt by dogs to control humans will also continue to rise. And, as long as dog owners continue to believe and behave as though their dogs are the same species as them and govern themselves accordingly, they will continue setting themselves up, and others for that matter, to be attacked by a creature of a different species that will bring interspecific aggression to bear against them. This deadly misperception and erroneous behavior on the part of dog owners has given cause to a very ominous statistic that will maintain equal pace with the rising dog population; nearly 50% of all dog bite fatalities result from the attack of a family dog.[8]

Protecting the young is a must for the perpetuation of any species, so the intense level of aggression associated with wolves in regard to <u>reproduction control & protection</u> has remained virtually unchanged with dogs as well. The biggest difference, other than the fact that a fertile dog can produce two litters a year compared to one by a wolf, thus increasing the possible occurrences of aggression, is who their pups need protection from. Nowadays, it's mostly humans and dogs that bear the brunt of momma dog's fury, and when they do, it is often fatal. In 2016, 29% (9) of dog bite fatalities involved active, or recent, breeding on the dog owner's property.[9] Thankfully, because of a rising participation in spaying and neutering by dog owners and animal shelters in the United States, the number wasn't higher. However, should that participation ever wane, it is almost certain that more dog bite fatalities resulting from reproduction protection will result.

Lastly, one of the most perplexing changes to canine aggression to come about through evolution and man's attempt to turn wild wolves into animals that serve his needs is one that is attributed to a blurring of the lines between aggression used distinctly for territorial defense and that used for interspecific control. Just in the years of 2015 and 2016, 15 of the 66 known fatalities that occurred to men, women, and children were caused by dogs that were either strays or dogs that had roamed well off of their property (territory), and none of the victims were eaten by the attacking dog(s). This begs the question of whether these human fatalities were the result of some sort of expansive territorial defense, or whether they were driven by the need to eliminate interspecific competition, even though a real form of competition did not exist between the victims and their attackers. I believe the answer is actually both, for the following reasons:

First, even though a wolf's territory is usually just large enough to provide resources needed for food acquisition and the rearing of cubs, the size of perceived territories occupied by dogs often exceeds well beyond the property lines of where they are housed by their owners. However, a great deal of territorial expansion by dogs is merely the result of an opportunity to expand, rather than an actual need or desire to do so. It often occurs when dogs are routinely walked a good distance away from their homes and are allowed to create scent posts (property claims) by urinating on various objects along the way. If their scent posts are not obliterated by the urine of other dogs attempting to take over or reaffirm the territory, they will soon perceive the expanded territory that they marked as theirs. In other cases, territories expand as the result of unrestrained dogs taking occasional extra-territorial forays, where they establish ownership of new territories the same way. Consequently, any land that is not actively being defended by a dog is subject to imminent domain by way of scent posting by any other dog passing through. Regardless of how it's obtained, dogs can afford to have such excessively large territories because energy conservation is not a concern for them like it is with wolves. They get fed by their owners whether they pee on every tree within five miles or not; whereas, with wolves, energy conservation is always a concern, and the size of the territory must therefore be economically justified at all times.

Second, some dog attacks may be related to food acquisition (killing prey), in that the dog(s) will attempt to consume their human prey after killing them, but such occurrences are extremely rare. In my many years of predatory behavior research, I have only been aware of a few fatalities in which the motive for the attack was clearly food acquisition. Such was the case with a family of four that was picking berries on an island neighboring Newfoundland, Canada, in August 1999. The family, consisting of a husband and wife and their two young boys, was attacked by eight Labrador Huskies that had been placed on the island to roam free during the summer months. The dogs stalked and killed the mother and the oldest boy and fed on their remains before the husband and the youngest boy could seek help.[10] Still, evidence has shown that nearly all domestic dogs involved in fatal attacks to humans discontinued what appeared to be the hunting sequence after the "kill" step, as was the case with Earl May. When Earl's body was discovered, there were multiple bite wounds to his head and torso, but there had been no attempt by Boss and Pete to feed on his remains. This type of behavior would be typical of both interspecific competition and territorial defense by wolves; the deciding factor being who the aggression is used against and where. For instance, if a wolf were to come into contact with a coyote, whether it was on its territory or not, the wolf would do its best to run down the coyote and kill it for the sole reason of eliminating an interspecific competitor. However, if a wolf were to come into contact with an alien wolf, where the contact occurred would have everything to do with the wolf's subsequent behavior. Off of its territory, the wolf would do its best to avoid the other wolf. On its territory, it would try to kill the other wolf for the sole reason of territorial defense. However, in both cases, the carcass of the dead coyote, or the wolf, would usually not be eaten because food acquisition was not the purpose of the aggression used.

For both of these reasons, it is quite possible that some of these fatalities occurred because the attacking dogs encountered non-conspecifics (humans) on their oversized territories and attacked them with either the intent to eliminate an interspecific competitor or to kill a trespasser. Both possibilities fit the characteristics of two distinctly different uses of the "Hammer"; therein lies the "blurring of the lines". Whatever it is, this strange new behavior by dogs is very real and it poses a great danger whenever humans encounter large unfamiliar dogs roaming loose.

There is little doubt as to the control that time has on all things. With enough time, a flowing stream will wear down a stone, but the remnants of the stone remain as minerals and sediment that are carried by the stream until they are deposited on a riverbed, where the process of forming a new stone begins all over again. Evolution is a never-ending process, and dogs have been evolving at the same rate as today's extant wolf, with neither resembling the creature they both originated from before the evolutionary fork in the road 40,000 to 60,000 years ago. Nevertheless, both the wolf and the domestic dog still carry minerals and sediment in the form of instinct from a time when both were one, and those minerals and sediment have fabricated the basis for how wolves and dogs behave today. For dogs, many of the intended uses of the "Hammer" by nature were either drastically reduced or eliminated through the evolutionary process and human-induced unnatural selection and behavior modification. At the same time, some of the uses were merely provided with a new object for the "Hammer" to hit, and in some dogs, it became muddled. As a result, the most significant changes that have occurred with dogs and their use of the "Hammer" is that humans have been added to the list of targets and most of the main purposes for which it was created have been whittled down to eliminating or controlling interspecific competitors, defending territories (regardless of size), and self-defense. Therefore, these three uses of the "Hammer" and how to prevent them from being used against us will be the main focus of this book. However, keep in mind that regardless of what the "Hammer" is used for by dogs, the intent of its creation, to kill or control another living creature through brute force, has remained virtually unchanged.

William Monroe

Willilliam Monroe, or *Wild* Bill as his partying friends from the 1980's still called him, wasn't like other men his age. He didn't dread the Holiday season like most of his buddies and didn't consider the decorating and shopping that came with it a hassle, like they did. In fact, he waited in anticipation for the five weeks or so that separated Thanksgiving and New Year all year long. He relished listening to the same Christmas CDs he'd carried around with him for over twenty years so much, he often listened to them outside the Holiday season. He especially enjoyed John Denver and Loretta Lynn's Country Christmas albums. Both seemed fitting in his three room, rustic cabin, located in the shadows of the Grand Mesa in Junction, Colorado. He loved baking dozens of chocolate chip cookies to give as gifts to his friends, and always baked a few without the chocolate so he could share them with his two Pit Bulls, Alice and Cooper, who could always be found sitting below the kitchen counter, waiting for the cookie dough that was sure to hit the floor whenever William baked. He loved the endless parties he was always the life of and even the ones he thought might enjoy his company regardless of whether or not he'd been invited. William had worked hard to cultivate his nickname, *Wild* Bill, and he took every opportunity he could during the Holidays to prove he still deserved it. Lastly, he loved decorating his cabin and the seven-foot noble spruce tree he always managed to snag before anyone else could make it to the Walmart parking lot on Warrior's Way to snag it first. Decorating was William's forte, and every year, it wasn't one second after taking his last bite of turkey on Thanksgiving Day before William was hauling his butt up the creaking, foldable ladder that led to his attic. It was there that thousands of Christmas lights and decorations, tucked away in plastic bins, waited for William to bring them back to life.

"It certainly is a wonderful time of the year," William mused, as he quietly sang along with the velvet voice of Andy Williams crooning from the vintage Kenwood speakers that were so large, their box frames took up eight **square-feet** of living space in his one hundred **square-foot** den. It was Christmas Eve, and he had just finished putting the last strand of blue lights on top of the magnificent spruce wedged in a corner next to the fireplace, when he noticed that one of the strands of lights near the bottom of the tree had gone dark. Most people William knew would've trashed the entire strand right then and there instead of taking the time to systematically check each bulb to find the one that had burned out so it could be replaced, allowing all of the lights on the strand to come back to life. But not *Wild* Bill. He treated each strand with a level of importance that most people wouldn't care to. Whenever he was asked why, he would always look away for a spell, but then he would shrug off whatever it was that had taken him away and say that it gave him more time to enjoy his two favorite Holiday pastimes; decorating and drinking. As if right on cue, Andy Williams delivered William's favorite line about toasting marshmallows. "And drinks for toasting!" William croaked a little late. "Darn it! Last time, I was right on target. Guess I'll need a few more drinks to help me get it right" he stammered. With that, *Wild* Bill took a sip of spiked eggnog that had slowly become more whiskey than nog, and set to work hunting for the one culprit bulb out of two hundred others that had waylaid his decorating.

William's love for the holidays would strike some folks as rather odd, seeing how he'd spent the previous six Christmases alone, ever since William's parents' car had slid off of I-75 and hit a stand of trees during an ice storm. In a twist of irony, his parents had been on their way to help William decorate the first tree of the Christmas season, to be purchased at the Walmart on Warrior's way in Junction Colorado, when they were killed. Ever since then, William had refused to depart from his family's tradition of waiting until Christmas Eve to decorate his tree, even though the tall, noble spruce had always seemed a bit out of place standing naked among the rest of the flashy decorations that had adorned his den each year since the day after Thanksgiving. Decorations like the plaid stockings filled with dog biscuits, raw hides, and cookies, which always hung from the fireplace mantle on either side of Williams' empty stocking. Alice and Cooper, the Pit Bull siblings he owned and adored so much he'd named them after his favorite rock star of his teenage years, were the only family he had left; and it was their plaid stockings that occupied the rusty nails his parent's stockings once had. A picture of William and his mother holding Alice and Cooper when they were puppies would always be found in its spot, centered above the stockings on the mantle. William had found the abandoned pups eating from an overturned trash can on Ute Avenue and, feeling sorry for them, had brought them to his cabin on Thanksgiving Day six years ago. The instant his father had snapped the picture, William's mother was caught with her mouth and eyes wide open; the physical result of her howling when Alice's sharp teeth had inflicted a playful nip on her left arm while being held for the picture. William's mother had objected to the photo, but the moment had remained frozen within the boundaries of a 4 x 6-inch frame portraying a scene of the Nativity ever since the accident. To hear his friends tell it, William's love for all the trappings that came with the Holiday season were his way of keeping the woman in the picture alive. After all, it was his mother's love for the music, the baking, and the decorating that nurtured William's love for it since he was a young boy, and if there was anything William had ever loved more than the Holidays, it was his mother.

It was while he was scanning the strand of lights that William's gaze landed on the exposed back end of his male Pit Bull, Cooper, who was lying with his front half hidden by a wall that separated the kitchen from the den. "Well, I'll be damned." whispered William in amazement. Earlier in the evening, William had purposely locked Alice and Cooper in his bedroom, as he had done each year when it was time to decorate the tree, because the two of them had always gotten in the way of his decorating by trying to un-decorate every chance they could. Looking in the other direction at the closed bedroom door, William leaned back on his sofa and pondered for a moment whether he was going crazy or, worse yet, if he needed to stop drinking. He had just about arrived at the conclusion that the latter would be the worse of the two when, to his relief, he heard Alice whimpering from the other side of the bedroom door in protest of being left out of the party. "If she's in the bedroom with the door closed, then how the heck did you get out"? William asked as he turned and looked back at Cooper. "He didn't get out you idiot, you forgot to put his sorry hide in there!" William scowled at the answer that came from his own mouth. Must have been good ol' Jack, from Lynchburg, Tennessee, that answered that question, he thought. "I might be crazier than an outhouse rat, but I'm no idiot." After all, no idiot could do justice to Christmas decorating the way he could. And with that, William winked at the noble spruce with seven hundred sparkling blue lights that were working, and proceeded to swagger toward the only half of Cooper he could make out, trying his best not to spill one precious drop of his drink all the while.

"Darn you, Cooper! That bone you're slobbering all over was supposed to be your Christmas present, and looky there, you done also tore up your sister's stocking!" yelled William as he took his eyes off of Cooper and peeked around the kitchen wall at two stockings hanging from the fireplace mantle instead of three. Exasperated and a little dizzy from the alcohol he'd consumed, William leaned against the refrigerator and took in the aftermath of Cooper's previously unnoticed delinquent activity. Almost camouflaged by the burnt orange linoleum covering the kitchen floor, were the many remnants of Alice's stocking and some of its contents. "That stocking's a goner, Cooper. It'll take a trip to

Walmart and another twelve bucks just to replace it. Not count'n what I put in it." William griped.

As he continued to run his eyes over the rest of the small kitchen, his gaze detected several out of place paw prints that ran along the counter top that lead to the other side of the refrigerator. "Ain't no way you done that!" chuckled an amazed William. As soon as he had seen Cooper chewing on one of the bones he had purchased for his dogs' stockings, he'd wondered how that fat boy of his had managed to get hold of it. After making his annual trip down to Montrose, where he'd previously paid a butcher friend for two of the largest bones he could find for his two dogs, William had set the prized bones on top of his refrigerator, where he figured it would be impossible for Alice and Cooper to steal them. "So much for that idea", William muttered as he shook his head. "Never knew you loved them bones so much you'd be willing to risk your fat butt fallen off that counter for 'em!" As if expecting Cooper to comment back, William turned his attention from the counter to the sight of his old boy lying ten feet away, licking and gnawing on the bone as though it were the last one on earth. "You're a darn pain Cooper, but I love you, so I'll forgive your thievery, especially with it being Christmas and all" he said to the big Pit Bull, whose attention and jaws were attached to one end of the large bone and not on William. "But, I'm still not going to just let you lay there and eat that whole bone. No sir, I'm not, so you best just give 'er up!" With that declaration, William pushed off of the refrigerator to go take Cooper's early Christmas present away from him. He knew Cooper wasn't going to be happy about having to give up his hard-earned prize. Last year, Alice had tried to take Cooper's bone away from him and had received seven stitches across her muzzle for her effort. "Would've been worse if I hadn't swatted your butt with that red-hot fireplace poker to get you to leave her alone." muttered William. "Yeah, you ain't gonna like it, but you still gonna be expecting a bone come tomorrow morning like always, and I ain't about to make that trek back to Montrose to fetch you a new one."

As William staggered across the kitchen floor and closed the distance to within a few feet of his dog, Cooper stopped gnawing on the bone and slowly raised his head. With his coal black eyes fixed on the approaching human form, the ninety-pound Pit Bull delivered a low, rumbling growl that carried an age-old warning known to competing predators. MINE! BACK OFF! The message was clear and uncompromising. William's advance and his breath halted simultaneously as instinct, as old as the Pit Bull's warning, stopped him in his tracks. *Don't move,* the instinct warned! Ushered from a place deep inside of William where premonitory suffering serves as the gatekeeper of human preservation, the warning was uttered with an urgency unlike anything William had ever experienced in his life. Like a helpless child, William obeyed the instinct and remained statue still, but Cooper continued to growl. Dumbfounded, William struggled to recognize the large dog lying on the floor with lifeless eyes and strings of saliva trailing from the pulled-back flesh that exposed its yellow fangs. He had heard Cooper growl at a few veterinarians, and during the time Alice had tried to take his bone from him, but never at William, and never anything like this. With each menacing snarl, Cooper's muscles twitched, reminding William of a lion he and his buddies had seen on TV that was lying in the long grass of the African Serengeti, waiting to ambush an approaching antelope. When the antelope had gotten within range, the lion had pounced on it. William remembered the cheers and the high fives he and his buddies had passed around when the lion snapped the antelope's neck with one bite. What William didn't remember was the remorse he was now feeling for the antelope.

There is danger! The instinct's hiss, acting like fine sandpaper rubbing the end of an exposed nerve, unmercifully jolted William from his self-reproach and redirected his attention back to a creature where remorse did not dwell. This can't be, reasoned William. It had to be a mistake! Cooper loved him and he loved Cooper, pure and simple, and because of that, there was no way his dog would ever hurt him. William wanted to vomit and cry at the same time, and for a second he thought he might do both. But, in a mighty effort to regain his composure and better footing on his sanity, he managed to stave off both and attribute the voice that he'd been hearing to the whiskey he'd been drinking for most of the day. "You're wrong, damn it! There's no way my boy would ever hurt me! I'm just drunk and that's all there is to it." And with that assertion, William took a step toward his dog. *HE'S NOT COOPER!* The instinct screamed with such force, William almost blacked out, and a few feet away, Cooper started to rise from the floor. *HE IS DEATH!* But, William no longer wanted to believe the voice. He only wanted to prove it wrong, so he continued to move.

MINE! Immediately, the message came again. But, this time, with a deafening roar powerful enough to drive the rising Pit Bull into an uncompromising stance over his bone. With fully-exposed fangs chattering slightly as a reflex to the blood pouring into the bulging muscles of his neck, Cooper began to advance toward William. MINE! The message, uttered by a species devoid of the same love humans have for one another, was no longer subtle. Instead, it was carried by a wave of amorality until it slammed into William's consciousness like a runaway avalanche. Ripping both his composure and his reasoning from his being, the avalanche hurled William's consciousness down a mountain of horror until it buried it in a suffocating blanket of fear. In that moment, William lost his way and reacted in the only way he knew how. He extended his shaking left hand toward the advancing dog. "Easy there, big fella. You don't want to spoil your Christmas morning, do you?" William forced himself to grin as he waited to see if his humor had any effect on settling his dog down. It didn't. Instead, William's outstretched arm had passed through an invisible gate and into a realm where survival was individual and reserved only for the fittest, and before William recognized his mistake, the gate slammed shut and Cooper attacked.

At the moment of the attack, a mechanism reserved for all those who face imminent death slowed time. It has been said that the slowing of time is God's way of showing us our lives. Giving us a moment to reflect, to say goodbye, or a last opportunity to ask for forgiveness. For William, it was none of these. Instead, it was sorrow played out in a slow, predestined inevitability as he stared into the fast-approaching eyes that would propel him to his fixed point in eternity. Eyes that betrayed all the years of love and sharing cookies, belly rubs, and walks along the Mesa's rim. Eyes that held no hint of gratitude for the sacrifices William had made to keep him and his sister. Like when he'd turned down a good paying job in Aurora, where neither Cooper or Alice were welcome because of breed specific laws. Like when his girlfriend of three years had presented him with the choice of *"me or them"*, or when he got laid off from his job and went without to make sure Cooper and Alice never did. No, there was no gratitude in Cooper's eyes. In fact, what really broke William's heart was that there was nothing in them at all. Cooper's eyes were as dead as the strand of Christmas lights William had tried to repair earlier in the day and, at the moment of his death, all William wanted was to find the burned-out bulb and bring the strand back to life.

"Remember William, just because one of the lights has died, it doesn't mean all of them have." The voice belonged to William's mother and she was standing beside him holding his hand like she had done so many times when he was a young boy. Together, they

were basking in the warm glow of nine hundred soft blue lights woven into the boughs of a magnificent, seven-foot noble spruce. *"The rest of the lights simply don't want to shine until they all can."*

In William's rustic cabin, resting in the shadows of the Grand Mesa, Andy Williams had just begun singing "Silent Night/Holy Night" when Cooper laid back down to finish his work on the bone.

Competitive Aggression -
The Evolutionary Rule of MINE

M any factors played a role in Cooper's deadly attack to William Monroe. The fact that Cooper was a dog that was strong enough to overpower William in a life-or-death struggle contributed to the tragedy. Love Pit Bulls or not, one cannot deny the tremendous muscle power and the crushing bite of the breed, plus the high level of aggressive response that was nurtured through selective breeding when mankind engineered a dog suitable for blood sports that included bear baiting and bull baiting. From 2005 to 2016, Pit Bulls killed 254 Americans, about one citizen every 17 days.[11] William Monroe would have stood a much better chance of surviving the attack had it come from a dog that did not share the same physical and mental attributes as Cooper.

The fact that the bone involved in the tragedy was no ordinary bone also contributed to the fatal attack. William had made it a point each Holiday season to procure the biggest and meatiest cow femur bones the butcher in Montrose had to offer. They were truly a prized possession for both dogs, as evidenced by the seven stitches Alice received from Cooper the previous year, when she had attempted to steal his bone, and Cooper's willingness to scale a narrow kitchen counter to reach one of them resting on top of a refrigerator.

The fact that William had been drinking most of the afternoon also contributed to the tragedy. Alcohol consumption is known for its ability to impair judgment, and its adverse effect on William's decision making and his awareness of the imminent danger he was in was obvious. Had he not drunk so much, his initial reaction to Cooper's first growl may not have been so casual, and he most likely would not have advanced toward Cooper after the dog's second and more powerful warning. Nevertheless, all of these factors, individually or combined, can be considered as nothing more than accessories to misfortune, or contributory negligence on William's part, but none actually give cause to Cooper's attack.

The acquisition and safeguarding of food, the sustainer of life, has always been the number ONE igniter of aggression on the planet earth, and it will always remain so. For without it, nothing else matters as brother turns against brother, predator turns against predator, nations crumble and kingdoms fall, and nature's creation withers away. Competitive aggression, the evolutionary rule of "MINE", an ever-present, never-indolent facilitator of any level of force required for food acquisition and safeguarding, gave cause to Cooper's attack. Its intrinsic selfishness gave no consideration to the fact that Cooper had been rescued, well-fed, and loved by William. Instead, it demanded of William, an advancing competitor from Cooper's perspective, an immediate withdrawal. When William failed to do so, and instead advanced, Cooper attacked. The ensuing struggle escalated rapidly until William, who was no match for the ninety-pound Pit Bull, succumbed to his injuries and died.

Selfishness - a concern for your own welfare and a disregard of others - is a distinguishing characteristic common in all true predators, even among those that form highly social groups, like wolves, lions, spotted hyenas, and African hunting dogs. The formation of social groups by predators was brought about by the need of individual predators to survive in an ecological niche that required the sporadic and provisionary support of other individual predators to obtain food that often came in the form of animals that were either much bigger, lived in large defensive groups, or were more dangerous than the individual predator could kill without jeopardizing its own safety. For example, wolves often work in a concerted effort to separate young calves from the protective herds of adult caribou, elk, and musk oxen so they can kill and eat it. Doing so requires precise teamwork and full reliance upon each individual predator to be unselfish during the "chase, catch, and kill" portion of the hunt to be successful. However, unselfishness, the very trait that contributes the most in providing the pack of wolves with life-sustaining energy at that moment, suddenly vanishes with the calf's last dying breath, and is replaced by the individual wolf's instinctive urge to ingest more meat than the other guy to ensure its own personal fitness. This selfishness, preceded by temporary unselfishness, also applies to the rearing of wolf cubs by the breeding pair. The same mother and father who unselfishly feed their cubs until they can fend for themselves, and who will readily attack a formidable grizzly bear attempting to excavate their den, are the same mother and father who will try to kill their offspring if they are caught poaching on their territory after they grow up and leave the pack. Driven by the law of limited resources, where "MINE" is the indisputable rule for staying alive, teammates and parents are forced to become individual competitors against the bloody backdrop of survival of the fittest.

This inherent selfishness, known as **competitive aggression**, is common to all dogs, and my research has revealed that it is the leading cause of dog attacks to humans. Some behaviorists and members of academia mislabel it as disobedience and mistakenly blame its actions on a character flaw created by a lack of proper training and socialization, while many dog owners who adopt shelter, or rescue, dogs make excuses for its ugly side effects because they believe their dog endured a previously abusive ownership and, as a consequence, is suffering from a post-traumatic-like condition. To these owners, the aggressive behavior of their dog is justifiable in their eyes. Nevertheless, all dog owners would rather believe almost anything other than believe that their beloved dog would ever be selfish enough to hurt them over food or an object, especially considering how much love, time and money most owners contribute to the relationship they have with their dogs. However, competitive aggression isn't personal. Instead, its selfish component is a natural trait that was passed from wolves to dogs and it continues to have a predominant influence on the behavior of even the most obedient, adequately socialized, well-fed, and abundantly-loved dogs. Coming to grips with this reality is the all-important first step in preventing its use against us. Fortunately, this shouldn't be too difficult for most people, because modern humans, the most invasive and exploitative social predators of all time, are all too familiar with the concept of selfishness. The only difference is that the human competitors slugging it out against the bloody backdrop of survival of the fittest are politicians, dictators, activists, corporate and economic leaders, religious fanatics, and/or anyone with access to social media. Other than that, it's the same evolutionary rule of "MINE," with individual humans using competitive aggression against other individual humans as a means of getting what they want.

Years ago, I was discussing this topic with a woman who was a renowned professor of anthropology and the owner of a very large Great Dane, who had bitten her through her hand when she had attempted to take a piece of trash from it, when it had picked some up while they were on a walk. I had already explained the concept of selfishness and its effect on predators and humans, and I was on my way to connecting the dots between the rule of "MINE" and the reason why her dog bit her, when she suddenly interrupted me and presented her own explanation. "Over the centuries, as we (humans) became magnanimous and a "put others first" society, we disassociated ourselves from its primitive, and very negative, connotation by labeling it (predatory selfishness) as 'self-preservation'. Meaning, nowadays, it's ok to be selfish like a predator only as long as you are saving yourself from harm. Otherwise, selfishness is frowned upon by modern humans because it is not in good keeping with the noble character we so greatly admire." Listening to her, I couldn't help but wonder how many kings or dictators throughout history had achieved their 'nobility' and their direct ascension to the throne by being a magnanimous conqueror? Saving that question for a later date, I continued to pay attention to her explanation. "Obviously, I have not demonstrated a noble character to my dog. I have been extremely busy with my work at the university and I now realize that I have failed to spend an appropriate amount of time with him. He was well aware that ingesting the trash was unacceptable and his bite was nothing more than his way of drawing my attention to my neglectful behavior. It's all really quite simple. He loves me and misses me when I am attending to my duties. It has become painfully obvious that I need to curtail some of my duties and make it a point to spend more time with him." Well said by a professor of anthropology, especially in regard to the "painfully obvious" part, but incorrect in its conclusion. Therefore, in my attempt to explain what really happened, I chose not to go on the defense and debate an esteemed faculty member of a major university. Instead, I went on the offense and fired a line of questions in rapid succession to keep the professor on her heels and drive reality into her intellectual but very illusionary skull.

"Please tell me again why you tried to take the trash from your dog?"

"Because I didn't want him to eat it." she answered.

"Why did you care if he ate it? After all, dogs eat stuff we don't want them to eat all the time. Stuff like socks, underwear, toys, human food, and even their own poop!"

"Because eating any trash can't be good for you, silly! Besides, there was something in the trash that appeared to be some kind of nasty meat. I love my dog and I didn't want the meat, or whatever it was, to make him sick." Her answer was accompanied by a sour squint over her bifocals. She was already becoming annoyed with my questioning, but I didn't let up.

Nodding, I asked, "Does he love you in return?"

"I am certain he does. I am all he has in this world." Her chin lifted three inches with her answer.

"If you are certain he loves you, then why did he bite you when you were simply trying to protect him?

"I have already explained why he bit me! He was upset because I had not been spending time with him and it was his way of drawing my attention to the fact. Otherwise, he would have readily given up the trash. He really is a good boy." The bifocals had come off and were now dangling on a chain around her neck. She was definitely annoyed!

Looking at the heavy bandage wrapped around her swollen, bruised hand, I wondered if she thought he had gotten his point across? Nevertheless, it was time to set the record straight, so I continued with my questioning while taking both the tempo and the tone up a notch.

"Professor, you are an incredibly intelligent woman. Do you really believe your dog nearly bit your hand off just to point out your absenteeism in your relationship?

The dangling bifocals slowly found their way back to the bridge of her nose. Peering over them, she regarded me with the same look that hundreds of students and faculty members must have endured over the years when she had peeled them apart, layer by layer, until they, and any thoughts or questions they had, were left naked and humiliated. Here it comes, I thought.

"No. Not really." she admitted.

No? Not really? I was shocked! I had expected a verbal beat down, but I was relieved when it didn't come. Fortunately for me, the esteemed professor had answered the question, not the dog's overly protective owner.

"Very good, professor."

No answer this time, but the look over the bifocals had lost some of its callousness. There was light at the end of the tunnel, so I decided to make a dash for it.

"When you tried to pull the trash out of his mouth, it was then that he bit your hand, correct?"

"That's correct. Although, the bite was more like a grab than a real bite." Now, the dog's overly protective owner was chiming in.

"A grab that punctured your hand clean through in two places and broke three bones, correct?"

The professor nodded as she reached for her damaged hand.

"What happened to the trash? Were you successful in taking it from him?" I continued pressing.

"No, it fell out of his mouth when he bit me. But, then he let go of me and snatched it from the ground and ate it. It happened so quick, I couldn't stop him. Besides, I was still in shock and I was afraid if I reached for it a second time, he would have bitten me again. His bite scared me and it hurt terribly." Looking away, she slowly lowered her bifocals for the second time. She was not only intelligent, she was strong, and did not want me to see the fear and pain that had suddenly betrayed her arrogance. The dignified woman who was one of the top minds in her field of study had been replaced by a vulnerable old lady that had suffered from competitive aggression. Slower now, I asked my final question.

"Were you being selfish when you tried to take the trash from your dog? He obviously wanted it more than you."

"Of course not, HE was!" But before her answer had settled in the air, she turned and looked at me as though I were one of the many discoveries she had uncovered in her decades of researching human behavior. After a few moments, she whispered, "Actually, I guess we both were."

Dogs are clueless of our good intentions whenever we try to take something harmful away from them that they wish to eat. Instead, they perceive our actions as those of a selfish competitor wanting to steal their prized food or object. We, in turn, perceive their attempt to bite us when we do try to take the harmful food or object from them as the actions of a spoiled, untrained, selfish brat wanting his or her way, or worse yet, those of a creature who has gone psycho! The former perception on our part is far more accurate than the latter. This is because food is never a sure thing for wolves, and with all dog behavior being anchored in the phylogenetic relationship they share with wolves, it's not a sure thing for dogs either. Some dogs will ingest a piece of trash as though it was the last morsel of food on earth, and they will attack anything, man or beast, that tries to stop them. Many of these types of dogs are the by-product of a former life on the streets, where nature's rule of "MINE" became self-evident as they found themselves competing against other homeless dogs, feral cats, raccoons, coyotes, birds, and rodents for an all-too-meager supply of food. Others are the result of a dominant genotype, and act more forcibly by nature because they just happen to have enough force in them to dominate the weaker dogs or humans they live with. Either way, these dominating dogs are typically well-fed, but will still attack anything, man or beast, that tries to take food away from them. It's not because they necessarily feel the need for more nourishment at the moment, but because they DON'T want their perceived COMPETITOR to have it. It's the same reason why a dominant wolf will drive his pack mates off of a large kill while he consumes up to 40 pounds of meat that he can't possibly digest at that time. After consuming the meat, the engorged wolf will sneak away from the other wolves, which are able to finally eat, and search for a place to hide his bounty. When he locates a suitable spot, he will dig a shallow hole and regurgitate up to 10 pounds of the meat into the hole and then bury it. He will continue the process until he has regurgitated and hidden enough meat to safely digest the remaining amount. By doing so, the dominant wolf has not only provided himself with a few extra meals, but by depriving his competitors of the excess meat, he has weakened their ability to overtake his position in the pack because they will be forced to use their energy to kill more prey for food instead of using their energy to challenge him. When acquiring enough food for survival depends upon the position you hold on a totem pole, you always want to be climbing up the pole or at least maintaining your current position, not sliding down it.

Nature infuses competitive aggression into the very core of the behavior of all predators as a safeguard of their existence. By limiting the number of predators able to survive persistent and fierce competition, she is able to control the delicate balance of predator and prey; thereby, keeping over-predation in check. Confronted with a scarce food supply, the weak perish under the competition's brutal pressure while the strong survive. The strong then go on to select strong mates, and their combined genes produce strong offspring that are born selfish; and if they survive long enough, they will grow to compete with each other and their parents for food and mates. It is the evolutionary rule of "MINE," and even after thousands of years of domestication, it still embodies the wild soul of today's dogs. If we continue to deny its existence, or fail to treat it with the respect it demands, we will continue to enter into deadly competitions with our dogs.

The Four Stages
of Competitive Aggression

Most people who are mauled or killed by a dog utilizing competitive aggression unknowingly enter into a deadly competition over food. However, it is important to know that the rule of "MINE" and its accompanying deadly aggression does not solely embrace food acquisition (for the sake of simplicity, I have lumped treats into the same category as food) and its safeguarding. It also encompasses the acquisition and safeguarding of a wide range of man-made objects, such as plastic and rubber bones, Kongs, tennis balls, stuffed toys, dog beds, and human furniture, just to name a few. Even things you would never think of, such as socks, underwear, pens and pencils, mulch, rocks, etc., can be included in the list. For instance, when I was a young boy living in Alaska, one of my sled dogs bit me over a favorite marble of mine! It was a Masher marble (twice the size of a regular marble) with yellow and black markings that made it look like a fat bumble bee without a head, and it was the envy of all of my friends who were playing marbles with me that day. While attempting to take out a friend's marble, my thumb propelled my Masher marble with such force, it ricocheted off his marble and sailed down the small hill in my backyard until it landed squarely in front of Annie, who was the sweetest of all the dogs I owned, if not the sweetest dog on earth. Well, at least she was right up until the moment I reached down to retrieve my marble which was resting two inches from her nose. It was then the Annie I knew and loved disappeared along with my prized marble. Some strange dog momentarily took possession of Annie's being and tagged me on my arm, and before I could scream, the strange dog let go of me and swallowed my marble whole. I searched Annie's poop for days figuring my Masher marble had to come out of her eventually, but I never found it. At the time, I was very sad about losing the big bumble bee Masher, but today, I realize I could have lost much more.

Without getting too wordy and too technical, what you could find yourself being bitten by a dog for is just about anything that the dog wants badly enough to fight you for it. In other words, William Monroe could just as easily have been attacked by Cooper for trying to take a ragged tennis ball or a wayward sandal from him as he was over a bone; although it is extremely unlikely that such an attack would have packed the same punch because the other objects would not have been as valuable to Cooper as the large, meaty bone. Nevertheless, with millions of dogs living with millions of humans in environments where they are constantly exposed to millions of different foods and objects on a daily basis, competitive aggression has become an unrelenting condition that sends millions of people to hospital emergency rooms each year and, sadly, a few of them to their graves. The good news is that it doesn't have to be that way. Avoiding becoming a victim of competitive aggression is relatively easy in that it isn't brought about by "crazy dogs" that suddenly and unexpectedly "turn" on people, nor is it brought about by the methodical plotting and execution of revenge by dissatisfied or jealous dogs. Heck, no one would be able to avoid competitive aggression if that were the case, unless they moved to an island not inhabited by dogs! Rather, the ontogeny of competitive aggression is a natural, four-stage process that serves to assist dogs in safely acquiring or keeping food, or any desired objects, from any perceived competitor. After accepting the fact that you could be attacked by any dog over any food or object, understanding the role of each stage in the development of competitive aggression is the second step in preventing yourself from becoming a recipient of its savage effect.

First stage (filter): Determining Value

The first stage of competitive aggression is the attachment of a value by a dog to any food or object to determine whether it's worth fighting for. This is the reason why labeling such behavior as "resource guarding" is not only incomplete in its description, but it's also negligible. When dog owners think of "resources", they typically think of food, not tennis balls, couch pillows, sticks, or any other non-food-like objects dogs enjoy. Consequently, their approach to taking such items from their dog is more careless than with food and they end up getting attacked as a result. Therefore, the use of the term "competitive aggression" is not only more accurate and realistic than "resource guarding", but it also places dog owners in the proper mindset so they don't let their guard down when they encounter it.

When dogs assign a value to food or objects, the higher the value assigned, the more it's worth fighting for. The lower the value assigned, the less it's worth fighting for. Therefore, reason stands that if we don't try to part valuable objects or delicious foods from our dogs, then we can avoid competitive aggression all together. Sounds simple enough, right? After all, it doesn't take a rocket scientist to figure out that if you try to take a big, juicy steak away from a dog, you'll probably get bitten. But, by the same logic, if you try to take a dirty sock, you probably won't.

If it is that simple, then why do so many people still get attacked each year? The reason is, WE do all of the assigning of value to anything our dogs possess and WE decide if it is worth fighting for, even though WE usually don't believe our dogs would ever fight us anyway. As a result, WE continue to get bitten year in and year out by dogs that continue to prove to us that THEY have their own valuation system and THEY are willing to fight us to acquire or defend anything THEIR valuation system determines is valuable enough! For this reason, it is crucial for you to understand that the assignment of any value to any food or object that would make it worth fighting for lies squarely with the dog and not you. Just because you don't think a particular item or food is worth fighting for doesn't mean your dog agrees with you. Case in point: One of the dogs my wife and I own is a six-year old Morkie (Maltese-Yorkie mix) named "Less Than Mighty" Dave. (He used to be called Mighty Dave, but the past few years have added a bit more heft to his waistline while at the same time, slowly eroding the "Mighty" half of his personality.) Regardless, my wife adores him, and he feels likewise; so much so that Less Than Mighty Dave accompanies her about the house no matter where she goes, even when she goes to the bathroom, and never had he shown the least bit of aggression to her until the day that he happened upon a miniature Hershey bar while following her around the house. When he did, it only took half a second for all the years of erosion to the "Mighty" part of his personality to be repaired! In the other half, he managed to draw blood from the one person on this planet that it appears he can't live without, even when all she wanted was to save him from the potential harm of ingesting the Hershey bar. Obviously, for Mighty Dave, keeping the chocolate was worth attacking the person who adores him most. As for my wife, she never believed her darling Morkie would ever bite her, especially over a miniature Hershey bar. But, as with my Masher marble and I, she learned otherwise. Fortunately for both us, the small price of our learning to always expect the possibility of being bitten when attempting to take <u>anything</u> away from a dog was negligible compared to the education it provided.

Second stage (filter): Cost vs. Benefit

The consideration of cost vs. benefit before taking any action is the universal standard for the success of any species. For wolves, survival is ultimately determined by their ability to consistently expend less energy and less wear and tear to their bodies than what is necessary to acquire more energy. It's why they prefer not to eat porcupines. Even when wolves are hungry, the cost of digging painful quills out of their muzzles for weeks and the lost time for hunting isn't worth the nourishment the porcupine provides! It's also why they will try to take down a large elk by grabbing it anywhere on its body other than the front end. That's because the front end of the elk has teeth, sharp hooves, antlers, and locomotion, which can stomp a powerful wolf into oblivion. Pain and suffering have always served as master teachers, and wolves learned quickly from both that the same benefit could be achieved with much less cost by grabbing the elk by the back end! Dogs, being domestic wolves, operate in much the same way. For instance, a dog chasing a squirrel will oftentimes, while being called by its owner, find the pursuit and the chance of catching the squirrel much more beneficial to it than the treat its owner is trying to coax it with, and not return. To achieve reliability in the dog's response to coming when called, its owner would have to insert a cost for not coming that would exceed any benefit the dog believes it would obtain for continuing its pursuit of squirrels.

The development of competitive aggression is also heavily influenced by the instinctual weighing of cost vs. benefit by dogs. All dogs involved in the process of attempting to acquire or defend anything of high value from a perceived competitor will weigh the cost versus the benefit of doing so before they commit to any action. If their initial assessment determines the benefit exceeds the cost, action on their part is almost certainly guaranteed. However, if the cost exceeds the benefit, they will abandon their attempt to acquire or defend the high valued item. For example, the Hershey bar that "Less Than Mighty" Dave discovered was no ordinary find. To him, it was like winning the lottery, and after his quick assessment of my wife, who was bearing down on him with the intent of taking his goldmine, he decided the benefit was worth the cost, so there was no way he was going to give it up to her without a fight. Even if it meant he had to bite the one person who loved him most. No offense to my wife, who is definitely not a "push-over", but when I demanded Mighty Dave's surrender of the coveted Hershey bar after he bit her, he immediately gave it up and didn't attempt to bite me. Apparently, the cost of doing battle with me versus my wife wasn't worth the benefit of keeping the chocolate bar.

In almost every case I have researched, competitive aggression never evolved from an upside-down equation where the cost far exceeded the benefit of acquiring or securing something of value. In the few cases I've researched in which the dog did not appear to give way to an obviously superior competitor, it was because the situation had morphed from competitive to self-defense in nature.

Third stage (action): Communicating Intent

No physical combat comes without a risk to either adversary. Even if one of the combatants is clearly outmatched by the other, accidents can and do occur. Wolves, who are extreme athletes that make their living by being very physical, can't afford such accidents. So, they developed a series of ritualized visual and auditory signals that are used to communicate their intent to attack before they actually do, in the hope that their warning will be heeded by their adversary, and thus allowing them to obtain their goal without a risky physical confrontation. More times than not, if the display is fierce enough, the "would-be" adversary decides that doing battle with such a demonic creature is not in its best interest and gives up. Therefore, after dogs have appraised the value of a particular object or food, and have decided whether the cost of acquiring or defending it is worth doing battle with their perceived opponent, they will attempt to accomplish their goal by using many of the same signals as wolves before they attack.

When William Monroe approached his dog Cooper, who was chewing on a highly-valued bone at the time, his advance communicated his possible intent to take the bone. To Cooper, that "possible intent" immediately transformed William into a "possible" competitor for the prized bone. Wanting desperately to keep the bone to himself, but also wanting to avoid physical combat with William, Cooper began to systematically emit a series of increasingly ferocious warning signals to stop William's advance. The first signal Cooper communicated to William was a hard stare - the "lifeless" eyes that William observed during the moments leading up to the attack. When his hard stare failed to stop William's advance, Cooper increased his warning by issuing a very deep growl and exposing his fangs. The addition of those signals temporarily succeeded in stopping William in his tracks. However, after a few seconds, William again began his fateful advance toward Cooper and the bone, which prompted Cooper to immediately escalate his warning even further by taking a position of straddling the bone and growling so viciously that his teeth chattered. William's continued failure to stop his advance, even after Cooper had intensified his warning to a very threatening level, convinced the big Pit Bull that a physical confrontation over the bone was unavoidable. It was then that Cooper began his own march toward William to close the gap to within striking distance. When William raised his left hand at the advancing Pit Bull, any "possible" intentions of him wanting to take the prized bone were affirmed by Cooper and he attacked.

The idiom, *shoot first, ask questions later,* may be put into action by brainless humans who fail to adequately ponder the outcome of their actions, but not by wolves, who have been made much smarter than humans in that way from the often-deadly consequences nature imposes on them for not heeding her advice to think before doing. Fortunately for us brainless humans, wolves shared nature's wisdom with our dogs, and because of that, you can always count on dogs to communicate a warning, albeit sometimes subtle, before they attack.

Fourth stage (action): Attack

With canine competitive aggression, the attack stage serves the sole purpose of physically driving competitors away from high-valued food or objects when visual and auditory warnings have failed to do so. For wolves, the duration and the intensity of the attack are typically just enough to accomplish the job. This is because, for them, a competitor for highly-valued food (a large kill in most cases) typically comes in the form of another pack member. Therefore, nature wisely installed a governor on their use of the "Hammer" in such cases to keep them from seriously injuring or killing one another, so that they can help each other kill large prey again in the future. In addition, a wolf's use of competitive aggression is restrained because the act of overcommitting themselves to winning a competition not only increases the risk of injury to both competitors, but it is also a huge energy-consumer for the victor. Many a wolf has learned a hard lesson when they overcommitted themselves to the job of vanquishing their adversary only to have a lessor, second competitor in the pack steal their bounty immediately afterwards because they were too exhausted to defend it.

For dogs, however, the rule of "minimal use of aggression to achieve the objective," when physically driving human competitors away from high valued food or objects, doesn't always apply for a few reasons. First of all, the domestication process has nearly wiped out most of the cooperativeness in dogs that comes with the provisional teamwork that is common with social predators like wolves, who count on pack mates to help with large kills; and instead, it has been replaced with an exaggerated form of the selfishness that rears its ugly head among wolves after the prey is killed and the assistance of teammates is no longer needed. This heightened increase in selfishness was created when we took a highly social and cooperative creature, the wolf, and turned it into a somewhat anti-social and much less cooperative creature that is today's dog. The effect of doing so has given cause to unnaturally fierce attacks by pet dogs under the influence of competitive aggression because, quite simply, they don't need the human competitors they are attacking to survive; somehow, some way, food keeps materializing in their bowls whether they seriously injure their competitor or not. Therefore, why hold back? Go hard and guarantee the win!

Secondly, when attacked by another dog that is physically superior to it, most dogs will try to run away from the fight. If they are unsuccessful in their escape attempt and are apprehended by their attacker, they will instinctually roll on their back and not move (their way of saying, "uncle"). In every instance of competitive aggression that I have witnessed, whether it involved a dog against a dog, or a wolf against a wolf, the attacking animal did not continue its aggression after its competitor clearly surrendered. That's because both behaviors are hardwired in canines. I give up and you let go...that's the deal. However, humans don't naturally surrender to aggressive animals. They may try to run away, like most dogs, but if they are caught by the attacking animal, their fear of being killed, seriously injured, or eaten by a creature they don't fully understand will propel them to fight back instead of yielding. Whereas, if they ever had a gun stuck in their face by an aggressive human demanding them to hand over their wallet or die, most would wisely give up and surrender their wallet. We would do this because as humans, we are hardwired to understand and anticipate the outcome of our actions with armed assailants that are also human. We are not, on the other hand, canine, and therefore we are not hardwired to understand and anticipate the outcome of our actions with attacking dogs. As a consequence, we are not sure that the attacking dog will let go of us even if we do give up, so we keep fighting to stay alive. Sadly, and ironically, our attempt at saving ourselves by continuing to fight only confuses our aggressor into thinking that we are still competing with them for the highly-valued food or object and as a result, our aggressor redoubles their effort to conquer us. In the vast majority of the fatalities I have researched, it was the continued fighting of the victims with their canine aggressors that was directly responsible for their demise.

If you own or interact with dogs long enough, you will eventually confront a dog who is willing to bite you to protect something they have, whether you want what the dog has or not. All that is required for you to become a competitor from their point of view, and to become vulnerable to an attack, is to simply approach or walk past the possessing dog at a distance that makes them uncomfortable and/or reach for their possession. Even so, competitive aggression doesn't happen spontaneously; for action taken by dogs to acquire or safeguard high-valued food and objects doesn't happen without purpose and analytic thinking being applied first, and the result being communicated to any perceived competition. Once this has been completed, the initiation of the fourth and final stage of competitive aggression will ultimately be determined by the actions of the perceived competitor.

Preventing Competitive Aggression

When dealing with any type of dog aggression, it is best to heed Jonathan Kozel's admonition to, *"Pick battles big enough to matter, but small enough to win,"* especially if the battle you're picking involves a dog operating under the evolutionary rule of "MINE." As explained in the previous two chapters, the acquisition and safeguarding of highly-valued food or objects by dogs is very serious business, and the "Hammer" that is used to take care of business typically enables dogs to win far more battles than they lose. With very small dogs, a loss of the battle on your part may not be too costly injury-wise, in that it may only require a few Band-Aids or stitches, but it will nevertheless cause you pain both physically and emotionally. Most of the victims who owned small dogs that attacked them admitted to me that the emotional pain of being bitten by a dog they loved, and had allowed the privilege of sitting on their laps and sharing their beds for many years, affected them more than the bite itself. Just as it is with a dear friend who has betrayed you, the loss of trust is oftentimes more painful and damaging than the act itself. However, if the battle ever pits you against the overwhelming power and abilities of dog breeds such as Rottweilers, Pit Bulls, German Shepherds, Mastiffs, Huskies, or the equivalent, emotional distress may be the least of your worries. With an average bite strength of the group measuring 269 pounds of bite pressure (Mastiffs topped out the group with 552, just short of the bite force of 600 pounds measured in lions),[12] most adult humans are no match for these types of dogs and they are subsequently seriously injured or killed by them. In a twelve-year period spanning from 2005 to 2016, these five breeds, or their equivalent, were responsible for 92.7% of the 392 dog bite fatalities.[13] To make matters worse, the aftermath of aggression by these breeds against young children is magnified tenfold compared to adults, with extensive plastic surgery and life-long physical and emotional scars as the minimum and death as the all-too-often occurring maximum. Unfortunately, when it comes to any type of canine aggression, especially competitive, the <u>behavior</u> of the opponent, not the <u>age</u>, is the determining factor for dogs when deciding whether to attack or not. Therefore, for our safety, and that of our young children, we must always be prepared to defend ourselves, and them, from the very real possibility that canine competitive aggression may be used against us. In order to do so effectively, we must learn what to do and what not to do should we ever find ourselves or our children in its deadly ensnarement. In providing direction on how to accomplish this, I have kept my guidance as simple as possible by limiting the information required to successfully prevent competitive aggression to only three steps. I did this because simplicity aids retention and retention aids proper execution, which is critical in averting an attack.

Step 1: NEVER assume a dog will allow you to take anything from it without a fight.

In the chapter titled "The Four Factors of the Attack" I addressed the fact that the vast majority of dog bite victims I have interviewed were people who had harbored the <u>disbelief</u> that they would ever be bitten by a dog, much less one that they owned. I went on to explain how their familiarity with a dog, their belief in justifiable provocation being required for an attack, and anthropomorphism, were major factors in the erroneous beliefs that eventually got all of them bitten. However, for the minority of dog bite victims I have interviewed, clear-cut stupidity was the major factor that caused them to be attacked, while for a few others, it was the misguided belief in being someone "special" when it comes to dogs.

I'm not sure what the reason for it is, but way too many people think they have a "special way" with dogs, especially with dogs they don't own, and that this "special way" makes them immune to the attacks the rest of us suffer. Regardless of the warnings being communicated by the dog and/or its owner not to approach, they'll saunter right up to the dog anyhow, while exalting their exceptional abilities the entire time. Alas, they won't get very far in reciting delusional phrases like, *"All dogs love me"* and *"I'm really good with dogs"* before they inevitably and painfully discover that dogs have their own "special way" of dealing with people like them.

Others find themselves being attacked for a somewhat similar "special" reason. The difference is that these people don't consider themselves to have any special talents in regard to persuading a dog to do their beckoning, but they do believe they enjoy a "special relationship" with their personal dog that makes them immune to being attacked by it. In other words, their dog may bite some other member of their family, but it won't bite them because of the exclusive, harmonic resonance the two of them share. As a result, their illogical conviction in a no-bite status, earned by their "special relationship" with their dog, eventually gets them bitten the same as those with a "special way".

There is no doubt that some people possess an uncanny ability to defuse hostility being permeated by some dogs, but not with ALL dogs. And, there's no doubt that some dog owners enjoy a very intimate, loving, and trustworthy relationship with their dog most of the time, but not ALL of the time. William Monroe had a "special way" with dogs, and the sacrifices he'd made for his two Pit Bulls, Alice and Cooper, gave evidence of a very "special relationship" he shared with both of them. Nevertheless, one of them killed him over a bone. Therefore, if ever you find yourself being confronted by a dog that is warning you of its intent to attack, it will serve you well to keep in mind that, at least at the moment, you're not the least bit "special". And if you fail to take the appropriate actions, you'll be attacked every bit as hard and as fast as the rest us, because with canine competitive aggression, there are no exceptions to the rule of MINE.

Dealing with canine competitive aggression is an initial success- or total failure-type proposition. It can strike <u>any</u> person, of <u>any</u> age, regardless of <u>any</u> "special" entitlements, <u>any</u> time that person and a dog are <u>anywhere</u> near <u>anything</u> the dog may want. Because of this, there is no room for <u>any</u> mistaken assumptions made by <u>any</u>one who finds themselves in the company of <u>any</u> dog.

Step 2: ALWAYS walk away from the fight.

If you should ever encounter a dog that is in possession of food or an object, and it is communicating warning signals of its intent to attack you, DO NOT step into the arena of competitive aggression.

Instead, immediately withdraw as the rule of "MINE" demands. The warning signals that are typically displayed by a dog before it attacks you include, but are not limited to, the following: *

a.   deep-throated growling

b.   a hard stare (the stare can be directed straight at you, or it can come from a sideways look. If that's the case, only one eye will be directed toward you and you'll see a white crescent moon on the side of the dog's iris similar to what you would see if a human were staring at you out of the corner of their eyes)

c.   pulled-back flesh on the muzzle exposing the dog's teeth

d.   ears laid back against the dog's skull

e.   hair on the dog's spine standing erect

f.   stiffening or trembling of the body

g.   tail-wagging or tail tucked underneath the dog's abdomen. The tail is the main signal provider for wolves and dogs, and its positioning and movement is used to convey their many states of emotional being, and/ or their intentions, to other wolves and dogs. In regard to any aggression, especially competitive, a wagging tail is NOT always an all-clear signal or a friendly invitation to approach the dog. Rather, it is most often an indication that the dog is still in the process of weighing cost vs. benefit and it may be conflicted in its ability to defend something of value from you. The higher the wag, the more confidence the dog has that it can take you. The lower the wag, the less confidence the dog has, and a tucked tail indicates the lowest confidence of all. That being said, don't get too comfortable with a low wag or tucked tail and attempt to bully the dog in an effort to make it give up whatever it's defending. Low confidence doesn't mean no confidence, and thousands of bite victims can attest to the fury of an unsure animal! In addition, even though these signals will be transmitted (individually or in a combination) by a dog prior to its attack, don't count on a dog giving you all day to recognize and heed them. If you recall, for aggression to be effective, it has to be fast, but for defense to be effective, it has to be even faster! However, when considering how fast is fast enough, it is best to regard Mahatma Gandhi's advice in that, "Speed is irrelevant if you're going in the wrong direction." Therefore, learn the warning signals, always be on guard for them, and be ready to act quickly, but correctly.

Walking away from a fight with a dog is always the best and most correct decision you can make regardless of the circumstances, but sometimes, there are occasions in which a dog involved in competitive aggression has in its possession food or an object that could potentially harm the dog if it is not taken. With regards to this, when given the choice of walking away or confronting their dog in such cases, most of the dog bite victims I interviewed said that walking away wasn't the option they chose, even though their dog clearly warned them not to approach. Instead, they risked being injured or killed in an altruistic attempt at saving their dog. However, the aftermath of their heroics proved to be widely unsuccessful and far more harmful to them than it was to their dogs. All of the victims suffered injuries, with half of them requiring medical attention, compared to no injuries, or lengthy veterinary stays, sustained by any of their dogs, who ended up ingesting or keeping the harmful food or object anyhow. These victims learned the hard way that the evolutionary rule of MINE trumps the selflessness that is common is such cases, and therefore, they are not likely to make the same mistake again. Nevertheless, I know that many owners who have not learned this painful lesson will still throw themselves on a grenade for their dog despite any foreshadowing of doom on my part, or any warning signals being communicated by their dog not to do so. Therefore, allow me to pass along a few points for you future heroes to consider that, hopefully, will assist you in arriving at the correct decision to not sacrifice yourself, or at least help you survive the blast with as little damage as possible.

First point of consideration: Do you really *need* to take the food or object away from your dog, or do you merely *want* to? The difference lies with *need* being assigned to those things that are possibly harmful to your dog, and with *want* being assigned to those things that are either not harmful, or much less harmful than those attached to *need*. Dogs assign different values to things they *need* (food) versus things they *want* (ball), and adjust their actions accordingly, and you should do likewise. If your dog is in possession of something you don't *want* it to have; e.g. large jewelry, articles of clothing, children toys, the leftover cheese pizza you left on the kitchen counter, etc., you need not read further because your best course of action would be to walk away and not risk being injured or killed by your dog for trying to take what it has. After all, any food involved will be gone in seconds, and any object will be discarded within a few minutes, or sooner, when something else appeals to your dog more. On the other hand, if your dog is in possession of something you feel you *need* to take from it; e.g. chocolate, poison, brittle bones, electrical cords, etc., you should still continue on to the next point of consideration before you dive on the grenade.

Second point of consideration: What is more important, your safety, or your dog's? Actually, this question demands an answer long *before* a grenade lands in front of you and you are forced to make a split-second decision as to whether to dive on it or not. Therefore, give your answer some thought so you'll be ready if or when the time comes that it is needed. While pondering your answer, also give some thought as to how those who love you would respond to the question on your behalf. I certainly know how a client of mine would have responded had he known that the Akita he and his wife owned was going to maul his nineteen-year-old daughter when she sought to take an oven mitt away from it. I still remember him tearfully saying to me, *"I don't know what's going to become of me. I never needed that stupid mitt, but I needed my daughter."* Sadly, the consequence of his daughter's decision to dive on a grenade for the sake of the family dog was not borne by his daughter alone.

Third point of consideration: Can you afford the price of trying to save your dog? A dog that is communicating a clear intent to attack you is a dog that has already analyzed the cost vs. benefit of keeping what it has (harmful or not) and it has decided that the benefit of keeping it is worth the cost of a physical confrontation with you. Consequently, what happens next, is up to you. If you withdraw immediately, the dog will have achieved its objective and you will NOT be attacked. If you continue with your attempt to take the dog's possession, however, you WILL be attacked and a price WILL be exacted in the form of injury, death and/or emotional trauma. The larger and more determined the dog, the higher the price that will be demanded. The smaller and less determined the dog, the lower the price. What you must decide is whether you can afford the price of your particular situation, and that answer is one that only you can make. If you decide that you can, then keep in mind that a successful outcome, one in which you are able to take possession of the harmful food or object from your dog without sustaining an injury, is possible, but not likely. However, if you decide that you can't afford to pay the price, then your course of action, albeit a very emotional one, is to withdraw and take solace from the fact that a potentially dangerous confrontation with your dog has been avoided.

Every time a person walks away from competitive aggression, that person ultimately wins. Their decision to do so may not be an easy choice, or one that accomplishes their goal of taking something (harmful or not harmful) away from their dog, but they will walk away.

Step 3: NEVER assume that you will win the fight.

This advice, in particular, goes out to all of the men who ignore Step 2 and let their testosterone get in the way of their good judgment whenever a dog growls at them or a member of their family. Oh, how I wish I had a dollar for every time a "man of the house" rebutted my advice to not engage their dog whenever it displays aggressive intent. If that were the case, my savings account would have probably earned some meaningful interest over the years. Even so, I can still see the swelling of their chests and hear the lowering of their voices when they all declared, *"There's no way in Hell I'm ever going to let a dog growl at me, especially one that lives in my house! Ain't no way I'm walking away! I'll kick his butt and show him who the real boss is!"* I was discussing this with an emergency room doctor one day when he remarked, *"Not a week goes by that we don't have to sew up one of those chaps. But, you should see the look on their faces after I finish mending them and hand them two prescriptions; one for their pain, and the other one for their hurt pride."* When dealing with competitive aggression, fellas, do what's best for your safety (and in any cases involving small dogs, the dog's safety), by swallowing your pride and walking away from the fight. Trust me, you'll both benefit from your withdrawal, and besides, this world can do with a little less pride in it anyhow.

Final thoughts

The acquisition or defense of highly-valued food or objects doesn't always result in a physical contest between a dog and its perceived competitor because in some circumstances, the competition is so one-sided that it never really becomes a competition at all. In the story of "Less Than Mighty" Dave and the Hershey bar, I was able to take the chocolate from him without a fight because competition for the chocolate never developed between the two of us. When "Less Than Mighty" Dave recognized my approach as that of a far superior creature with the intent of taking his prize, he never growled, showed his teeth, or attempted to compete with me in any way. Instead, he quietly gave up his prize and walked away. In the wild, no competition = no competitive aggression = no one gets hurt, and looking after number one is the number one rule. "Less Than Mighty" Dave followed the rules and played it safe by not competing with me for the chocolate. You should do the same. Never compete with a dog that wants to compete with you.

Lastly, a great deal of competitive aggression can simply be avoided by not allowing ourselves to be placed in a position of having to compete with our dogs to either save them from harm or to save something we value from them. This can easily be accomplished by making sure harmful food or objects, along with our valuable possessions, are kept safely out of their reach. In other words, if you wouldn't leave it out for a toddler to get ahold of, then don't leave it out for your dog. My Grandfather once told me, *"Sloppy people are sloppy at everything they do and as a result, things in their lives tend to get real messy at some point."* Don't be a sloppy dog owner, because competitive aggression can become real messy, really quick.

Competitive aggression doesn't have to be the leading cause of dog attacks to humans, because what is required to prevent it is well within our capacity. We just need to have the watchfulness that comes with believing that we can be victims of it. When we believe, our watchfulness will warn us of its presence, and then our knowledge of why and how it develops will guide our decision-making and actions so that we escape harm. Hopefully, you can do this now.

---

* See Appendix A - Canine Warning Signals

Sara McAlister

Bo's Garage was set back a ways off of Hwy 431, the main roadway that connects the small rural towns of Wedowee and Roanoke, Alabama. Located midway between the two municipalities, the auto repair shop had enjoyed a robust business back in its heyday, fixing the cars and trucks that belonged to nearly everyone living in both communities and anywhere in between. However, the last twenty-five years had not shined as much on the garage's good fortune, with fancy new shops, all sporting the latest in automotive diagnostic and repair equipment, springing up all over Randolph County and competing for business. It didn't take long for the wealthy patrons of Bo's Garage, seduced by the shiny Art Deco flooring, flat-screen TVs, air-conditioning, and free donuts that the other shops offered, to realign their auto repair loyalties and ditch what was once the only auto repair shop within 30 miles of their upper-middle-class homes. Afterwards, the only patrons of Bo's Garage were the ones who couldn't afford the prices demanded by the shops that offered the free donuts, or the no-good thieves that took every chance they could to hop the six-foot, rusty, chain-link fence surrounding the auto graveyard in the back to steal parts off of the fifty or so decomposing cars. That is, until Bo Bailey, the seventy-six-year-old proprietor of Bo's Garage started turning three large male Rottweilers loose within the confines of the chain-link fence every time he left work. From then on, only the same lower-class drivers looking for high-class bargain repair jobs frequented Bo's Garage, and all of the thieves looking to steal car parts stayed away.

Sara McAlister was new to Wedowee, Alabama, and at the moment, she was also very lost. "Where on God's earth is this place?" she muttered while anxiously scanning both sides of Hwy 431. The address for Bo's Garage, written on a yellow Post-It Note by her father that morning, served as her GPS because her cell phone hadn't picked up a signal ever since she'd left civilization, which, in her opinion, was only ten feet southeast of Wedowee's city limits. The fact that it was not quite daylight yet didn't help matters much either, but she had pleaded with Mr. Bailey to take a look at the truck she was driving on a day his shop wasn't usually open, and he had been kind enough to grant her request. "If you can come by at 6 am on Sunday, that'll give me enough time to take a crack at fixing that old truck your father won't part with before I go to church. Speaking of parts, I just about used up all the parts I had the last time it was here. I certainly hope I have what it needs. I know how ornery your father can be and how much he favors that damn truck of his, even though it barely runs." "And, so do I," answered Sara out loud to herself as she strained to make out anything resembling a mailbox, sign, or driveway that belonged to Bo's Garage. With each passing mile and each shriek she heard coming from the engine compartment, she was becoming increasingly worried that the truck she was driving was going to explode into a fountain of cracked vinyl, discarded beer cans, and corroded steel.

The truck was an old, beat up, 1991 Dodge Ram Pickup that belonged to Sara's father, who took every opportunity he could to remind her that the "disgusting" truck, as she had regrettably called it after one of the times it had broken down and left her stranded, was not only paid for, but was also the truck she had ridden in on her way home from the hospital where she was born. He would also take every opportunity he got to point out the fact that it was his "disgusting" truck that had also carried Sara home from the emergency room where she had been treated for a near-fatal overdose of crystal meth when she was fifteen years old and from the drug rehab center where she'd stayed for three months afterwards. If those examples of her lack of gratitude for his truck weren't enough for Sara to feel like she'd been run over by it, her father would also remind Sara that it was his "disgusting" truck that had recently picked her up, along with what little possessions she owned, from the apartment in Birmingham, Alabama, she had been evicted from for not paying her rent. With the truck loaded down with a dresser, a chair, two mattresses, and Sara's last forty dollars, which he'd taken for gas money, he had driven her to his home in Wedowee, where, as he reminded her, she was currently living "free of charge." Whenever Sara used the truck to get to her new job at the local hardware store, or to go to the laundromat, or to the pharmacy to pick up the medications she took for her depression, she could count on her father taking advantage of his graciousness to convey his contempt for her and her apparent inability to get her life together. Ever since his wife had divorced him, citing his abuse of her and his drinking problem (which she blamed) for Sara's drug overdose) as the cause, he had developed a grievance toward his daughter and would use anything he could, like her dependence on him for the past few weeks, to prey on her vulnerability as a means of assuaging the perpetual self-pity that drowned his soul. So, after the old truck had quit running a few times, with one of the times resulting in her receiving a stern warning not to be late for work again, Sara had grudgingly asked her father to have the truck repaired. The next morning, when he'd given her $300 and a Post-It Note with the address to Bo's Garage, Sara knew it wasn't out of the goodness of his heart that he did so. Rather, she believed his actions were motivated by a distorted sense of self-worth that demanded he feel needed by her, and feeling needed by anyone was something he hadn't felt since the time her mother had slammed the door on his "disgusting" truck and had walked out of his life.

He wasn't always like that, thought Sara, as her hands alternately went from gripping the steering wheel of the truck to wiping the tears that had suddenly formed in her eyes. She could remember a time when he would come home from his job at the lumber mill on the north side of Birmingham and let her pull out the splinters that would inevitably find their way into his large, calloused hands each day. He would screech and howl with every poke of the tweezers and pretend he couldn't take her "torture" any longer. In the beginning, Sara was mortified and thought she was hurting her father, but after the first few times, she caught him winking at her mother and knew his act was just a put-on. Afterward, every time he howled, she would giggle and admonish him for being a big baby. Sadly, it wasn't but a few years later that the lumber mill shut down and the splinters were soon replaced with whiskey bottles, and the winks to her mother were replaced with insults. Listening to the screams that filled their home daily was too much for young Sara, who hid under her bed reading Cinderella over and over again, praying that a young prince would come riding a pumpkin carriage to rescue her. However, six years later, it wasn't a prince or a pumpkin carriage that came for Sara. Instead, it was a freckle-faced teenage boy from down the street with crystal meth and a St. Vincent's Hospital ambulance, and by the time she was released from the drug rehab center, it was a drunk and broken man driving a beat-up truck. Since then, it seemed to Sara that every turn she'd made in her life had led to a dead end, and that was what she was thinking when she finally recognized the address to Bo's Garage spray-painted on a wooden plank nailed to a telephone pole, and made the final turn of her life.

Bo Bailey loved his three dogs. Even though it cost him a hundred bucks a month to feed them, he figured it was worth it because ever since he'd gotten them, none of the spare parts still attached to the wrecks in his salvage yard had come up missing. "Good thing you boys love me too, but it took y'all a bit to come around," Bo reflected as he filled bowls of food from a metal storage bin located in the shop's small kitchen. "Too small for all three of your fat butts, that's for sure!" Bo declared to the three dogs, who were slobbering all over themselves in anticipation of an earlier than usual Sunday breakfast. Brutus, a massive, 120-pound male

Rottweiler, along with his two slightly smaller siblings, Rambo and Tiger, had originally belonged to a friend of Bo's until the day a stray had run up on his friend's property and the three dogs had shredded it like a log going through a wood chipper. After that, his friend's wife had become worried that a friendly stranger would just show up like the stray dog did and be shredded the same way, and had demanded the three dogs find somewhere else to live. Judging by the reaction Bo had gotten from the dogs the first couple of weeks after his friend had backed his pickup truck up to the gate to the fenced enclosure and let them loose, he would have agreed with her.

For a few days, Bo wasn't confident his new acquisitions were going to work out. Brutus, who was meaner than snake spit, would hit the chain link fence like a runaway freight train while Rambo and Tiger tore at it until their mouths bled, trying to get at Bo any time he went near them, and leaving him with the initial impression that the auto parts they were protecting would remain every bit as inaccessible to him as they would to any potential thieves for the foreseeable future! Nevertheless, the three dogs finally came around, and even started enjoying the occasional scratches behind the ear that Bo would offer on the days his arthritis didn't flare up. It wasn't long after that that Bo added on to the existing fence until it butted up to the back of the garage, which the local thieves had resorted to breaking into when they weren't able to steal parts from the salvage yard, and let his dogs guard that too by also installing a large dog door that gave them access to the shop's interior. From then on, Brutus, Rambo, and Tiger roamed the inside of the fence and the shop with deadly precision from the close of business until they were put back on their chains just one minute before the shop opened the next day. Because of that, word soon spread all over Randolph County and anyone who ended up with the first appointment of the day at Bo's Garage knew never to arrive there more than a minute early.

However, Sara was new to Randolph County, and she was still learning her way around, so it wasn't unexpected that she turned onto the gravel driveway leading up to Bo's Garage more than ten minutes early. It was just plain bad luck. And, as bad luck would have it, her arrival coincided perfectly with the loud slurping and crunching that typically occurred while the three dogs ate, so none of them, including Bo, ever heard the old, "disgusting" truck laboring up the driveway. It wasn't until Bo heard something crash in the lobby and what sounded like someone crying out, that he became aware of Sara and remembered he had invited her to come by at 6 am so he could look at her father's truck before going to church. "Oh, dear God," he whispered as the tiny clock on the microwave glowed 5:51 am. Ever so slowly, Bo looked down at his three dogs; praying they had been too preoccupied in devouring their food to have noticed. But, Brutus had already turned his head in the direction of the front door, and Bo watched, horrified, as his muzzle inched upwards, revealing strands of saliva and bits of kibble wedged between his teeth. Bo instinctively reached for the massive Rottweiler, but in less time than it had taken for his brain to register the futility of his action, Brutus, Rambo, and Tiger raced out of the small kitchen in a flurry of flying bowls and kibble. The whirling of the stainless-steel bowls, with their contents hurling in every direction, suddenly reminded Bo what a log looked like when it came out of the other end of a chipper, and the thought of Sara being the log made him run.

"Thank goodness!" Sara yelled. When she had turned off of Hwy 431 and onto the driveway leading up to Bo's Garage, the truck had started lurching, and the shrieking from the engine had become so loud, Sara thought a part of it was going to break off and sail straight through the driver's compartment and impale her! Now, as she brought the truck to a stop in front of the garage, she hoped Mr. Bailey would be able to resurrect the old truck and bring it back to life. Not because Sara had grown attached to it, but because the next day was Monday and she needed the old beater to get her to work so she wouldn't lose the job that would hopefully provide her with the means to move out of her father's house someday. "Wouldn't that be something?" Sara asked herself as she dabbed her eyes with the last tissue she had remaining and climbed out of the cab.

Sara was almost to the front door before she noticed the "Closed" sign hanging on the inside of the door. A quick glance at her watch revealed she was 10 minutes early. "Maybe, I beat him here," Sara muttered as she scanned the small gravel parking lot and the driveway leading back to Hwy 431 for any sign of Mr. Bailey or his vehicle. Seeing several old cars and pickups scattered about the property that could have belonged to anyone, but no sign of Mr. Bailey, Sara reached into her pocket and pulled out her cellphone to check the signal in case she needed to call him. "Damn," she hissed at the No Signal notification, "might as well not have a phone in this backwoods county!" After stamping her feet a few times in frustration, Sara tucked the phone back in her pocket and looked around for something to sit on while she waited. She had just about decided that one of the tar-coated railroad ties that served as parking bumpers would make a better choice than getting back in the truck, when she was surprised by the sound of clanging metal coming from a dimly-lit area of the shop. Turning slowly in the direction the sound had come from, Sara held her breath and strained to make out what she had heard. Almost immediately, the clanging came again, but this time, it reminded her of the time her mother had given a hungry stray dog some food. Her father had strictly forbidden the dog from being taken in the house, so Sara's mom had fed it in the garage. The dog's licking and groveling ended up pushing the stainless-steel bowl over every square-inch of the concrete floor, in his attempt to get every last morsel of food out of it. Remembering how the scraping sound of the bowl on the concrete had made goosebumps stand on her skin, Sara smiled for the first time that day and moved closer to the front door. As she bent over to peek through the one windowpane on the door that wasn't cracked, she distinctly heard the sound again. "It has to be Mr. Bailey. He must've gotten here before me", she reckoned. Incredibly relieved, Sara glanced up at the heavens and whispered "thank you" as she reached to turn the knob.

It was only after the door opened that Sara was able to see the three dog houses that sat under the outstretched limbs of an "American Sweetgum" tree, outside the back of the building. The houses were enormous and filled the frames of the windows that lined the lobby's back wall. In front of them, rusty chains the size of Sara's arm were held in place by thick metal stakes driven deep into the bare earth. Four-inch wide leather collars adorned with sharp spikes were connected to their ends with padlocks. Having been raised in Alabama, Sara was used to seeing dogs owned by poor people chained to all sorts of things, including trees, cement blocks, tractor tires, and even broken-down cars. The poor couldn't afford nice fences, so they chained their dogs to anything they couldn't drag off to keep them from escaping. Still, she had never seen chains used to secure a dog that were as big as the ones she was looking at, and she couldn't imagine what kind of dogs required them. 'My gosh, they must be huge!' Sara muttered in astonishment. She also wondered where they were. The thought of three enormous dogs running loose somewhere on the property worried Sara, but she assumed they were safely behind some sort of fence. However, something else about the entire scene wasn't right. Something was missing and it wasn't just the dogs. She couldn't put her finger on it, but whatever it was, it had her deeply concerned, so she moved a few feet closer to the back windows to take a better look.

At first, Sara didn't notice the flooring of the lobby when she took her first steps, partly because of the room's poor lighting and partly because her attention was focused out the back windows, but when her left foot snagged the leg of an end table, she cried out in pain and looked down to see what had inflicted it. In an instant, a bone-crushing panic hit Sara, and she felt her pulse quickening as she remembered the scraping sound that had drawn her to the front door and how it had reminded her of the stray dog pushing a bowl of food around their garage. Fighting to control the panic that threatened to consume her, Sara prayed she was mistaken, but when she bent over and touched the floor, the cold, smooth surface was unmistakable, and Sara instantly realized what had troubled her about the dog houses and their chains. There were no food bowls.

By the time Sara realized the scraping sound she had heard were metal bowls being pushed across the floor just a few feet away, she was already out the door and racing for the safety of her father's truck. A mere second later, Brutus rounded the corner of the small kitchen, with Rambo and Tiger not far behind. As she ran, she could hear the big dog growling and the thunder of thousands of small pebbles being kicked up by his paws and ricocheting off the garage's tin siding. The truck was only a few yards away, but Sara could already feel the hot breath of her pursuer on the back of her legs and knew the dog was right behind her. Sara screamed and fought to go faster, but Brutus, who had inherited the will of one of the most successful and prolific predators of all time, willed himself to go even faster, and when Sara's outstretched hand finally reached the truck's door handle, he launched.

In the driver's window, Sara saw the reflection of Brutus' massive head and exposed yellow fangs as they rose over her left shoulder and knew she was going to die, but at that moment, she didn't think about her death, or watch as the terrible reflection loomed closer. Instead, her eyes fell upon a pair of tweezers that were tied to the keychain that still dangled from the truck's steering column. Sara hadn't noticed them when she had taken the truck's keys from her father that morning, but she had observed an unusual look in his eyes and sensed some sort of change in his demeanor. At the time, she'd chalked it up to the aftermath of drinking an entire bottle of whiskey the night before, but now, gazing at the tweezers, she knew it was something she hadn't seen in many years. Sara knew it was love, and her mind had already retaken her to a time when those very tweezers had brought so much delight to her and her father, when Brutus slammed into her body with such force, the impact caved in the driver's door and drove Sara's head through the window, killing her instantly.

Bo Bailey never made it to the church that day. By the time Sara's father left, and the police and the county coroner finished their investigations and carried Sara, the truck, and his three dogs away, the last worship had concluded four hours prior. "That's ok. God doesn't love me no more after today anyway," Bo moaned as he sat on an upside-down bucket, staring at the blood stains that outlined where the truck had been parked when Sara died. He shuttered at the memory of his three dogs tearing at Sara's body and how they would have done the same to him when he tried to get them off of her if he hadn't grabbed a pitchfork on his way out of the shop. When Sara's father asked him how his daughter had died, he wasn't able to say anything to him. There were no words to describe what he'd witnessed. "No one deserves what she got," Bo muttered. "No sir, no one. Especially that girl."

The sun's rays were settling on the rows of pine trees that grew on the west side of his property when something yellow caught Bo's attention among the varying shades of crimson. But, because he was sick to his stomach and didn't want to do anything for the time being, he just sat on the bucket and tried to figure out what it was from his vantage point. Nevertheless, after a few minutes, he became tired of guessing and with a sigh, he pushed off the bucket and set off to find out what it was. When Bo got close, he could tell it was a yellow Post-It Note sticking up out of the blood-coated rocks. Bending over, he carefully prodded the note with his pitchfork and discovered it was two Post-It Notes stuck together. As is typical with the popular square notes, the adhesive that binds a hundred or more of them together had bound the two. Plucking the notes out of the blood-covered rocks, Bo wiped them off with his hands and pulled out his bifocals so he could read what was written on them. After studying both notes for several moments, he took off his glasses and wiped his eyes with one of the handkerchiefs that could always be found in the left back pocket of his overalls. On the top Post-It Note was written the address to his garage. The one underneath held a message from Sara's father. "I think I might have a splinter or two that needs pulling when you get home if you're up to it?" "Well, I'll be damned," Bo whispered. Before the truck that Sara had driven was towed away, her father had asked the police if he could take something from it. At the time, Bo recalled reading about how people didn't always act right during such moments of grief and thought that Mr. McAlister might have been having one of those episodes when he saw him pull an ordinary pair of tweezers off of the keychain. It wasn't until Mr. McAlister looked up from what he was doing and saw Bo staring at him that he tearfully explained why he'd wanted them.

In the distance, several dogs were giving chase to something, and Bo turned his head to listen to their frenzied barking. "There's more death in the air," he thought, then shook his head and walked back to his garage. When he got to the front door, which had remained open since the tragedy, he reached inside and made sure the CLOSED sign was facing the parking lot and in view of anyone who approached the garage. "That's how it's gonna stay," Bo said quietly. Then he shut the door and headed for the one vehicle in the parking lot of Bo's Garage that still ran.

Territorial Defense - The Invincible Center

In the wolf kingdom, a territory is a sociographical area that is aggressively acquired and defended from conspecifics. Each territory serves mainly as a resource for food, a habitat for courtship and mating, and a safe dwelling place to raise the young. Always taking cost versus benefit into account, the size of the territory is normally just large enough to provide a wolf pack with the space to accomplish all three needs while still being economically defensible. As the surrounding area the territory occupies becomes denser with other wolf packs establishing bordering territories, attacks to neighbors become more frequent and fierce, as boundaries are challenged and vital food resources are pillaged by trespassers. In his book titled "On Human Nature," Edward O. Wilson describes how territories under such conditions eventually develop an "invincible center" that is defended *far more vigorously than intruders attempt to usurp it, and as a result the defender usually wins. In a special sense, it* (the resident) *has the "moral advantage" over trespassers".*[14] For wolves, the "invincible center" is the denning site (small location for whelping cubs), or the rendezvous site (a small area occupied from mid-summer to fall and used as a rearing place for quickly-growing juvenile wolf cubs and as a place for adults to rest and meet), and both locations are defended with greater violence and determination than the far-off, outer lying areas of their territory. For pet dogs, the "invincible center" is the house or apartment, and the yard or lot where they live, sleep and are fed, and their territory can encompass any surrounding area, up to several miles distant, that they frequent when being walked by their owners or when they roam loose. And, just like it is with wolves, their "invincible center" is more aggressively defended than the other regions of their territories.

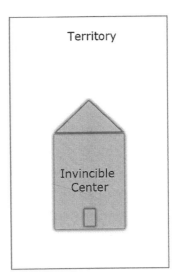

However, where pet dogs mostly differ from wolves defending their "invincible center" and territory is who they have to defend theirs against. In the case of wolves, it's mostly alien wolves and the occasional marauding bear, but with dogs, it's usually an unfamiliar human who is unaware he or she is trespassing on the dog's territory. When Sara McAlister stepped into the lobby of Bo's

Garage, she had no clue she was encroaching on the "invincible center" of a territory that, for years, had been vigorously defended by three very capable Rottweilers. By the time she saw the empty, oversized doghouses and chains in the back lot and realized their implication, it was too late. Brutus, Rambo, and Tiger had detected an intruder that had breached the perimeter of their "invincible center," and subsequently ran Sara down and killed her like they had done to a stray dog that had committed the same offense on a different territory they had occupied a few years previously. It didn't matter to the three dogs that Sara was a nice girl and that she was there by invitation of their owner. It didn't matter that she had no intention of stealing anything, whether it was their food or otherwise. It also didn't matter that their owner had done a good job of making sure all of them were well-fed and would have continued to do so if the tragedy hadn't occurred. What mattered, was that Sara was not known by the three dogs, so her presence inside of the "invincible center", made her an immediate threat to the vital resources contained within. That is what mattered to the guardians of Bo's Garage and it continues to matter with every single dog in every single home or apartment, because territories provide the best opportunity to stay alive and prosper as a social predator. And, because it mattered so much, Brutus, Rambo, and Tiger, upon detecting Sara, imposed the same penalty on her that wolves impose upon alien wolves that attempt to breach their "invincible center". That penalty was death.

The continuance of the instinctive urge to kill trespassers in dogs like Bo's three Rottweilers is mostly the result of a strong, dominant genotype that was passed from wolves to dogs and exploited by mankind in some dog breeds, like the Rottweiler. However, because of its hereditary roots, it can be found in any dog, regardless of its breed. Wolves that possess such genotypes are always the more dominant and higher-ranking wolves of the pack, and higher-ranking wolves, because of their supreme power and determination, are the gatekeepers of the all-important "invincible center," while lesser duties are delineated to the weaker lower-ranking wolves. According to Alaska Department of Fish and Game wildlife biologist Tom Meier, *"Wolf packs in Alaska may be a symbol of true wilderness to many people, but in some respects, they resemble inner-city gangs. Each wolf pack has a pair of leaders, the alpha male and female. Each pack has a territory, or turf, it marks and defends. Fights between packs are common - and often deadly. More often than not, it's the alpha males or females that are killed* (during territorial fights), *because they're the ones out front doing the fighting."*[15] Dogs that inherit the same dominant character trait will guard their "invincible center" as seriously as any alpha wolf, and as a result, they are more likely to inflict a harsher penalty on trespassers compared to dogs that inherit weaker and more submissive genotypes that are common with lower-ranking wolves. Hence the reason why Bo, after losing valuable auto parts to thieves for years, chose to augment the fence surrounding his salvage yard with three large Rottweilers, who had already proven that they were willing to shred trespassers like a log going through a wood chipper, than with three dogs of much lesser drive.

Fortunately, the instinctual drive to impose the death penalty on trespassers has faded somewhat with time and man's benevolence, and it is no longer common to all dogs. However, with territorial defense being the second leading cause (competitive aggression being first) of dog bite fatalities in the United States, many dogs have tragically demonstrated that the drive to kill trespassers has not faded as much as we would like to believe. On the contrary, the urge to completely annihilate humans that threaten to encroach upon "invincible centers" is still inherently potent enough that the number of human lives lost to canine defenders of territories would undoubtedly surpass competitive aggression if all dogs possessed the same size and strength of an adult Rottweiler. But thankfully, mankind didn't stop with just his manipulation of wolf genetics for behavioral reasons in dogs. He also stuck his fingers in the pie of morphology and significantly reduced their size and power. As a result, even if the instinctual drive to kill a trespasser is still very strong in some dogs, not all of them have the physical ability to accomplish the task. For instance, if Sara McAlister had been attacked by three very-determined Yorkie defenders instead of three very-determined Rottweilers, she would have very likely survived the attack. Still, whether or not a dog has the desire to kill a trespasser or the physical ability to do so, mankind got his hand slapped by nature when he tried to alter some inherent survival instincts, like territorial defense. Consequently, all dogs are still instinctually driven to protect their "invincible center" from unfamiliar humans. The means by which they do so, and the level of aggression they use, varies with each individual dog, but even so, they will defend their "invincible center" until the unfamiliar human is either killed or driven away, they (defenders), are killed or driven away by the unfamiliar human, or the unfamiliar human is eventually accepted by them.

One way of defending the "invincible center" that is utilized by a great many dogs that find a physical barrier separating them and the trespasser, is to put on a mighty show of deterrence. By growling and barking, while at the same time charging the doors or windows of the house or the perimeter fence like a four-legged madman, they are able to drive most perceived trespassers away. This is often the case with strange people passing by, or with deliveries being made to the dog's territory. The show put on by dogs doesn't always start off so menacingly, but because these types of intrusions tend to repeat themselves, and oftentimes by the same perceived trespasser (usually people in uniform - U.S. Postal Service, UPS, FEDEX, etc.), dogs feel the need to up the ante in their aggression on account of their previous attempts at running off the same trespasser having apparently failed. Whenever a delivery is made to our home, for instance, a huge spectacle of viciousness on the part of our dogs is guaranteed to greet the delivery person. In the beginning, when our dogs were younger and the number of deliveries numbered less than a few dozen, they would mostly just sound the alarm to announce the intruder's presence by barking or woofing. Nowadays, after several years and several hundred failures at running off the same intruder for good, our dogs will hurl themselves at the front door with every atom in their bodies until the same trespasser (delivery person) kindly sets the package by the door and leaves our territory. Afterwards, they'll strut their stuff for a few minutes and beg me to congratulate them on finally getting the job done, while I, on the other hand, just shake my head and wonder why some dog owners persist with the notion that dogs are little humans. After all, even the dumbest human would eventually realize it wasn't their actions that made the delivery person leave their territory. The delivery person left, regardless of the behavior of the territory's defender, because he or she had more deliveries to make to other territories! But, because dogs are not little humans, they never manage to see it from that angle, and so they continue with their ever-escalating show of aggression until the doors, windows, or fences, which have borne the brunt of their numerous assaults, give way on their own, or by their owner's mistake, as was the case in the tragic deaths of Sara McAlister and Earl May. When this happens, someone usually suffers from the other way dogs defend their "invincible center".

In 2014, the year which Earl May was killed, loose dogs straying from their owner's property inflicted 40% of all fatal attacks.[16] Needless to say, when exceedingly vicious dogs the size of Boss and Pete no longer have cheap chicken wire holding them back from defending their "invincible center," or oversized chains in the case of Brutus, Rambo, and Tiger, trespassers can expect to receive something far deadlier than a mighty show of deterrence. At a minimum, they can expect to incur severe injuries if they are not able to escape or prevent the dogs from assaulting them. When wolf packs encounter other wolf packs in the wild and there are no natural barriers separating them, a fierce and often deadly battle for territorial rights is almost certain to ensue. Wildlife biologist Craig Gardner, who has studied wolves in Alaska for 22 years, has observed some *"pretty good rumbles,"* and studied their aftermath. One particular outcome of a rumble he investigated involved significant losses to two wolf packs fighting over territories south of Fairbanks in October, 2009. According to Craig, a wolf pack previously identified as the Tatlanika pack had traveled over 40 miles from their territory when they encountered the Clear Creek Butte wolf pack. The resultant brawl left many of the wolves dead, including the alpha male and female from the Clear Creek Butte pack. *"All we know is they left with 15 wolves three or four days before the fight and they came home with nine,"* Gardner said of the Tatlanika Pack. The Clear Creek Butte pack, meanwhile, had decreased from 13 to nine wolves. *"It looks like a bomb went off in both of them,"* Craig said. *"I've never seen it where it looked like a hockey fight. It looked like they all just dropped their gloves and went at it."* Even smaller, or less vicious dogs, when not physically restrained, will "drop their gloves" and inflict physical injuries to people who they feel are encroaching on their territories. But because of their size, the injuries trespassers receive are usually not life-threatening or fatal. Nevertheless, with human populations growing denser and online sales growing, established territorial boundaries surrounding "invincible centers" will continued to be breached by greater numbers of unfamiliar people, resulting in higher numbers of people who will suffer attacks from unrestrained dogs of all sizes. In 2016, the United States Postal Service reported

6,755 of its employees were attacked by dogs nationwide, which was 209 higher than the year before.[17] In the same year, the United Parcel Service (UPS) said 900 of its delivery drivers suffered dog bites as well. The cause? Unfettered dogs defending their "invincible centers".

Defense of any territory that provides life sustaining energy and protection for offspring is crucial to the survival of wolves. It is the same with humankind. A quick history lesson on your part will reveal how crucial territorial rights and protection have been to the millions of people who have taken lives, or given their lives, for its cause in countless wars. Is it no wonder then, if wolves and humans find defending their territory so vitally important to their survival and well-being that they're willing to kill for it, that dogs would feel the same way about their territories? The answer is yes.

Zoo Keeper - Preventing Territorial Aggression

Years ago, while running in rural Alabama, I was simultaneously attacked by four dogs and became a victim of territorial aggression. The incident occurred at a time long before smartphones guided us from point A to point B in our everyday lives. But, having grown up in the Alaskan wilds, I felt confident about my abilities to navigate unfamiliar lands unassisted by the use of technology, so I laced up my shoes and headed out from the hotel where I was staying to get in a good run and scout the surrounding area. I had been running for several minutes on a gravel road I'd discovered a few miles from the hotel when I spotted a trail leading into the woods. Because I had already spent so much of my life in remote wildernesses and couldn't turn down the opportunity to explore a new trail, I changed course and proceeded down the narrow dirt path to see where it would lead.

Normally, you wouldn't have caught me running or hiking without my trusty bear mace, but because the trip was sudden and the airlines had not allowed me to take a canister of incapacitating spray on the plane, I didn't have it with me when I rounded a bend about a quarter of a mile into the woods and suddenly came upon a clearing with four shacks, all resting atop stacks of concrete cinder blocks. For me, the adventure of trailblazing has always resided in the journey and not the final destination. The vast changes in the terrain, elevation, and fauna that I have encountered while hiking on primitive trails that have crisscrossed mountains, jungles, and rainforests have consistently made for more challenging and inspirational moments than where the trails ended up. However, that sentiment changed abruptly when two very stout Pit Bulls and two German Shepherds charged out from under the shacks, all of them hell-bent on vanquishing the idiotic trespasser that had just run into the heart of their "invincible center!"

I have been charged by enough predators in my life, including wolves, bears, lions, and dogs, to know when the tactic is a show and when it's not. When a group of wolves stumble upon a dangerous competitor, such as a grizzly bear eating its kill, if they're hungry, they will try to harass the bear enough to make it give up its meal. The tactic they utilize is called "bluff charging," a maneuver in which they make quick, but ferocious, feints at attacking the bear, but not actually engaging it. The tactic is often successful, but sometimes it has deadly consequences when a feigning wolf zigs when it was supposed to zag and a well-timed swipe from the irate bear crushes its skull. In the previous chapter, when I wrote that dogs would defend their "invincible center" until the unfamiliar human is either killed or driven away, or they (the defenders) are killed or driven away by the unknown human, I meant it. The attack I was suddenly under by the four dogs was no bluff charge, and there was no way they were going to stop until I was dead. If I were going to make it back to my hotel in one piece, I would have to become a grizzly bear and drive them away from me. Realizing that, I swooped up an old tree branch that was about five feet long and as big around as my forearm that was lying on a pile of other branches and debris next to the trail, and commenced swinging it at the charging dogs like a crazed bear! As ill-advised as it may be to attack an animal that's attacking you, sometimes it works, and it certainly did for me on that day. My first swing connected perfectly with the skull of the lead Pit Bull while he was lunging for my throat, and before the sound of the crack vanished in the air, I followed up the hit with a savage thrust to the second Pit Bull's face that stopped him dead in his tracks. Out of the corner of my eye, I saw one of the German Shepherds dart in to take a bite out of my right calf. I whipped the branch as I spun around and managed to deflect his bite with a glancing blow to his muzzle that was hard enough to send him scampering away to a distance safely out of reach. Looking quickly for the other Shepherd, I saw it cowering several feet behind the one I had just hit and knew that it wanted no part of the fight, so I spun around again to look for the two Pit Bulls that had led the attack. Halfway through my spin, I felt the one that I had jabbed in the face try to latch on to my left leg with his powerful jaws, but fortunately, it was winter time and the lightly-insulated running pants I was wearing caused him to grab more material than leg. But my relief was short-lived, as I felt him jerk and thrash my leg in an attempt to pull me to the ground like a wounded deer. I knew in that instant that my survival depended upon my remaining on my feet, where I could wield the branch in my hands as an effective weapon. Otherwise, if I were pulled down, the mighty branch would become useless and the four dogs would overpower me within seconds. At that moment, all sense of time and the morality that came with being a human vanished as the animal within me that wanted to live took over. I cocked the branch and let loose a primordial scream that hearkened back to a time when survival of the fittest by man was accomplished with makeshift clubs like the one I held, and then I swung the club with all my might at my opponent. On impact, the big branch broke in half, but my assailant went down hard and let go. The first Pit Bull that had taken a substantial hit to the head with my first swing of the branch was back on his feet, but he was dazed, and his resolve to fight me had considerably diminished in his eyes. Nevertheless, I knew that once he regained his composure, he would be after me again, and I wasn't about to give him the opportunity to do so. Screaming at the top of my lungs, I charged him. The hunted had turned into the hunter, and the big Pit Bull, suddenly realizing he was outmatched, tucked his tail and ran back to the shacks with the other three dogs trailing behind. The message communicated by my last scream that said that I was not going to die that day had not been lost unto any of them.

It wasn't until my attackers had sought refuge back under the dilapidated shacks that I realized I'd had an audience the entire time. One of them was a woman holding a baby, and only their faces were visible as they peaked out from behind the partially-opened door of the shack nearest me. The other spectator was an elderly man, who was watching from behind a screen door that was barely held in place by leather straps, in the shack furthest away. Neither of them moved or spoke a word. They just stood there staring as though the life and death struggle that had just played out in front of their homes held no meaning to them. I stared back, but I wasn't able to detect even the slightest trace of sympathy or concern for my safety in their eyes. It was like looking at humans that had died a long time ago, but their bodies had refused to acknowledge it. With chills running down my spine, I slowly backed away from the clearing and headed back to my hotel, still clutching what remained of the big tree branch that had saved my life.

The memory of the attack that threatened my life still haunts me, but I shouldn't have to live with that memory. Why? Because,

I can sum up in ONE sentence what it would have taken to prevent what had happened to me, and what it will take to stop other people from becoming injured or killed by dogs defending their territories. **BE A GOOD ZOO KEEPER.** Come to grips with the fact that you own a domesticated social PREDATOR that still has powerful jaws with teeth that are attached to a neck designed to carry its offspring for miles and drag animals down that weigh up to 10 times its body weight, and treat it like one instead of treating it like a surrogate child. Wolves aggressively defend their territories. Dogs aggressively defend their territories. In doing so, wolves attack wolves, and dogs attack people and other dogs. Both use their powerful jaws and teeth that are attached to powerful necks as tools to repel or kill trespassers. Neither uses police officers, security guards, mediators, or attorneys. Wolves don't always respect the territorial boundaries of other wolves, and dogs don't always respect property lines. When wolf cubs grow up and move away, if they are ever discovered on their former territory by their parents, they will no longer be considered as family. Instead, they'll be considered as trespassers and treated accordingly. If your dog has not been given the opportunity to meet some of your family members or your dog hasn't seen them in a couple of years, if they are discovered on its territory, they'll not be considered as family either. Instead, they'll be considered as trespassers, and could be treated accordingly. If you visit social predators such as wolves, lions, or African hunting dogs at a zoo, there will be chain-link, steel bars, thick acrylic panels, or a combination thereof separating them from you. This is called "good zoo keeping" and it's for your safety. When strangers visit your home or they are given access to your property, you have to safeguard them from your social predator as well. You have to be a good zoo keeper until you are <u>certain</u> your dog has accepted them.

Being a good zoo keeper also applies to guard dogs, personal protection dogs, or any dog that could be classified as a dangerous dog. According to Charlotte Walden, Michigan State University College of Law, dogs can be defined as dangerous if *"the act or actions of a dog puts the public or other animals at risk for injury or death".*[18] She goes on to list how many states have used the following categorizations to define dangerous dogs:

- Engages in or is trained for animal fighting
- Aggressively bites, attacks, or endangers, or has inflicted severe injury on a human being on public or private property
- Bites a person unprovoked, causing an injury
- Kills a human being
- Injures a human being
- Severely injures or kills a domestic animal, which may include livestock, while off of the owner's property
- Has, when unprovoked, chased or approached a person upon the streets, sidewalks, or any public grounds in a menacing fashion or apparent attitude of attack
- Aggressively attacks in a manner that causes a person to reasonably believe that the dog posed an imminent threat of serious injury to such person or another person although no such injury occurs; provided, however, that the acts of barking, growling, or showing of teeth by a dog are not enough.

I am not an attorney, but I would strongly advise that you consult with one well-versed in home and business owner legal responsibilities required of the state in which you live or operate a business before you acquire a personal protection dog, or turn a guard dog loose that has the same determination to kill and dismantle trespassers as Brutus, Rambo, and Tiger did. Just because you own a dog for the purpose of protecting your assets or your family, doesn't automatically negate your responsibility to keep non-criminals from being attacked by them. The judicial right to use lethal force, whether the force is generated by a weapon or a dog, requires a clear and present danger to your personal safety or that of your family before it is employed. Utilizing a guard dog to protect your personal or business property requires a clear and present intent of criminal activity on the part of the trespasser for its judicial use as well. The problem lies with the fact that the latter use is more susceptible to non-criminal human error than the former. Such was the case with Sara McAlister. It wasn't just Bo who had witnessed Brutus, Rambo, and Tiger charging the chain-link fence surrounding the back of his property like a runaway freight train. More than a few residents of Randolph County had visited Bo's Garage and had seen the same thing, while other customers had observed the three dogs straining so hard against their enormous chains that they, unlike Sara, who couldn't believe the chains were so big, couldn't believe the chains were so small! However, Sara's visit to the garage was her first, so she was not aware of the three dangerous dogs that were currently being utilized by Bo to protect both the inside of his repair shop and the salvage yard that was outside. Therefore, she entered the front door of Bo's business with no more hesitation than anyone else would have. After all, who would expect to be attacked by three dogs for entering a place of business a few minutes before an appointed time?

Lastly, in addition to everything else, there were no BEWARE OF DOG or NO TRESPASSING signs, or any other warning notifications displayed near the lobby entrance that may have prompted her to knock on the door instead of opening it and stepping inside. Consequently, because of an unlocked door that should have been locked, no warning signs about the guard dogs posted within view of the entrance, and three dangerous dogs that were not physically restrained, Sara ended up walking into a death trap instead of an auto repair shop.

From a theft prevention standpoint, Bo's choice of dogs was a sound decision, and one that is made by many property owners before or after they suffer from the damaging effects of thievery. However, owners of such dogs are charged with the responsibility of preventing them from attacking legitimate customers that frequent their businesses or invited guests to their homes. Although Bo had been very diligent in his duties of keeping his customers safe from his dogs for many years, he eventually failed one of them and <u>he</u> was answerable for the tragedy, not his dogs. In her article, *"Dog Owner Liability for Bites: An Overview"*[19], attorney Mary Randolph states that dog owners can be found liable for their dog's actions and face civil and criminal prosecution if even one of the following three are true:

1 **The owner knew the dog had a tendency to cause that kind of injury—the "one-bite rule."** This misleadingly-named rule makes an owner legally responsible for an injury caused by a dog if the owner knew the dog was likely to cause that type of injury—for example, that the dog would bite. The victim must prove the owner knew the dog posed a danger.

2 **A dog-bite statute makes the owner liable.** State dog-bite laws make owners responsible for almost any injuries their dogs cause, whether or not the owner knew the dog had a tendency to cause that kind of injury.

3 **The dog owner was unreasonably careless, and that's what caused the injury.** If the injury occurred because the dog owner was unreasonably careless (negligent) in controlling the dog, the owner may be liable.

In Bo's case, he was definitely guilty of two of them. He knew his dogs could, and probably would, kill anyone trying to steal parts from his salvage yard or break into his shop, which was located in Alabama, a strict statute liability state. As for being unreasonably careless, I don't believe he was. Instead, I think that the concept of Murphy's Law came into play. We are all familiar with this adage, which states that if anything can go wrong, it will. If your dog has previously shown a high level of hostility directed toward any unfamiliar people who have visited your home or property while your dog was physically held back from them (door, window, fence, leash, etc.), should you fail in your zoo keeping duties, like Bo, there is a good chance that Murphy's Law will be enacted and someone will be attacked by your dog(s).

When I use the term, "be a good zoo keeper," I am not implying that you necessarily own a dangerous dog that needs to be re-homed to a zoo, or that you need to keep your dog behind bars all of the time. Rather, what I am implying is that all dogs possess the potential to attack perceived trespassers when it comes to defense of their "invincible centers," and because of this, precautionary measures (good zoo keeping) should be taken by you in the form of some sort of **physical restraint** until your dog proves that he or she is comfortable with your guests and will not bite them. For extra clarification, yelling "NO," "STAY," or "BAD DOG," at your unrestrained dog does not constitute good zoo keeping, regardless of how loudly you yell it! Neither does asking your guest to hand treats to your dog as some sort of conciliatory attempt at making friends while your unrestrained dog is growling or trying to nip them. Every year, thousands of dog owners subject their guests or the service people who visit their homes to the unnecessary risk of being bitten because they mistakenly believe treats trump trespassing. Most dogs that aggressively defend their territory or their "invincible center," don't give a hoot about treats until the trespasser either leaves or sticks around long enough to earn your dog's acceptance. The amount of time that will take will be determined by your dog and not by you, but if you are familiar with your dog's behavior, you should be able to easily recognize when it occurs. In the meantime, maintain complete control of your dog's actions in every instance of strangers paying you a visit. Even if your dog has accepted the stranger in the past, continue your control until your dog gives you the "all clear" signal. My preference for accomplishing this is by one of the following methods:

- **Leash your dog**. Make sure the leash you use is 4-6 feet in length and has good integrity throughout its length. Also, ensure that it is attached to a non-slip collar so your dog doesn't back out of it. DO NOT USE A RETRACTABLE LEASH to restrain medium to large size dogs! Way too often, either the thin cord attached to the connecting clasp breaks or the mechanical brake fails, and the victim, who was standing several feet away from the dog, is still bitten. Keep in mind that even a non-retractable leash will grow a few feet in length as soon as your powerful dog causes your bent arm to straighten when it lunges.

- **Kennel your dog**. Dog kennels come in various sizes, shapes, construction material, and prices. Of all of the choices you can make, the most important one is the construction material. Make sure the kennel you choose is sturdy enough to keep your dog in when it tries everything it can to get out of it! Also, don't always trust the manufacturer's latching mechanism that is supposed to keep the kennel's door from being opened by your dog. Instead, if your dog is extremely aggressive toward visitors, take the extra step of supplementing the latching mechanism with additional securing hardware. Lastly, if your visitor brings a small child, place the kennel in a separate room and shut the door. This will prevent the child from sticking their fingers in the dog's kennel, which constitutes as a breach of both trespassing and self-defense to your dog and the consequence for some children in the past has been an immediate amputation of the encroaching fingers by the dog.

- **Board your dog.** Sometimes, the best way to deal with something is to not deal with it at all. I highly recommend boarding your dog at a commercial dog boarding facility, or at your veterinarian's clinic if they offer boarding, whenever you expect a lot of visitors arriving in a short period of time (as in the case of a large party or family reunion). The greater number of strange people you have in your home at the same time, the greater the likelihood that 'Murphy' will be one of them, especially if alcohol is being consumed. Besides that, the loud screaming and laughing that typically accompanies a great deal of parties is very unsettling to most dogs. Do you and your dog a favor by choosing not to deal with territorial aggression at all. By doing so, you can enjoy your party and your dog can enjoy not being a part of it.

Methods that I <u>do not</u> prefer for good zoo keeping and physical restraint:

- **Using baby gates**. Child safety gates (baby gates) are intended for keeping human children between the ages of six months and two years away from potential dangers. What they are not intended for is keeping attacking dogs, who are much more powerful and strong-willed than small children, from being a potential danger to your guests. Even if their flimsy construction is capable of holding back your dog, you still have to trust that your guests won't reach over the gate to pet your dog. Trust me, some people think they can do that and get away with it. Sadly, when they fail, they end up blaming you.

- **Placing your dog in a separate room or in the back yard without using a kennel.** How many times have you thought you closed a door when you actually didn't? How many times has a guest asked to use your bathroom and mistakenly opened the wrong door while looking for it? How quickly can young children leave your sight and open doors? How many times have you become distracted by your guests and forgot your dog was standing behind the door you were about to open? Lastly, how often has your dog managed to open the door by himself? If you've learned anything from Bo's mistake, you won't trust an unlocked door to safeguard your guests from your dog ever again. The potential for human error is just too great.

- **Trusting obedience training before it can be trusted.** For many years, I have helped dog owners establish reliable responses to given commands. While doing so, I was sure to preach the importance of training for the condition. For instance, if you don't want your dog to pull you when it sees another dog while walking, after teaching the fundamental skills required of walking with humans, you will need to practice walking your dog in the vicinity of other dogs. Otherwise, your dog won't learn that the requirement to not pull you while being walked also pertains to dog encounters. Simply stated, if you wish for your dog to be reliable in its response to a command while under a particular condition, you will have to train your dog under that very condition. The problem with training your dog to "stay" while under the condition of people trespassing on its "invincible center" is that it's either initial success or total failure in the beginning, when the training process is still immature. Nevertheless, you will never have a reliable response to "stay" when visitors arrive unless you train under that condition. That being said, go for it, but be sure to start your dog's training with a good back-up, like a leash in your hands, just in case your dog feels its training can wait until after the trespasser is made to leave.

No matter which method you prefer for good zoo keeping, never allow your dog's small size to dissuade you from the necessity of it. Of the 74 dog bite fatalities that occurred in the U.S. between 1966-1980, two of the dogs involved were a Dachshund and a Yorkshire terrier.[20] Therefore, the same attitude and approach used to physically restrain medium- to large-size dogs from attacking perceived trespassers needs to be adopted with miniature- and toy-sized dogs as well. When Mark Twain declared, *"It's not the size of the dog in the fight, it's the size of the fight in the dog,"* he was spot on. Little dogs don't consider their size when they confront trespassers. If anything, they'll throw more of themselves into the defense of their territory than most big dogs! Because of that, when I used to visit client's homes where I knew miniature or toy dogs were waiting for me, I would provide some of my own protection by wearing the thickest socks I had. Good zoo keepers don't take into account the size of the predator they are entrusted with when keeping visitors safe from them, and you shouldn't either. Whether you own large dogs or miniature dogs, be a good zoo keeper and treat them all the same when it comes to protecting people visiting your home or business.

There are no absolutes or universal truths involved in keeping everyone safe from territorial aggression. Dogs are animals and their perception of who is a trespasser and who isn't may not jive with our human perception. Many dog owners have been left scratching their heads when they tried to figure out why their watch dog watched all of their stuff leave with burglars without doing anything about it, but then tried to bite the police officer that stopped by to write the report. Territorial defense by dogs is also fluid in that territories contract and expand as dogs age or are given more freedom to roam, or when their territories are supplanted by new ones when their owners move and take them with them. And, despite our best efforts at being good zoo keepers, accidents will occur; 'Murphy' wouldn't have it any other way. However, we must continue to try.

The attack that occurred to me in the woods of rural Alabama and the one that occurred to Sara McAlister have both been the driving force behind my writing about territorial aggression. Sara died, but I survived, because God placed a mighty limb at my feet and my adversaries were not Brutus, Rambo, and Tiger. I can only imagine the horror Sara must have felt, because had I been forced to fight her three killers, instead of the four that I did, there would have been no branch mighty enough to save me. Even still, I can't shake that day. I continue to suffer from its crushing effect every time I hear a dog growl, or see a dog that resembles one of my attackers. In my sleep, I have fought the battle a hundred times over. In several of them, there is no limb to save me from the dogs who tear at my throat while the people in the shacks just watch with no pity and do nothing to help me. Because I suffered and continue to suffer, I am a victim of territorial aggression, and so are Sara and anyone else who has been needlessly attacked by the dogs of irresponsible and reckless owners who failed to be good zoo keepers. If Sara or I had been afforded just a smidgen of the control and preventative measures that I write about in this chapter, it is likely neither of us would have been harmed. However, we weren't. When I ran the wooded trail leading up to the clearing and the four shacks, there were no BEWARE OF DOG or NO TRESPASSING signs to warn me of any possible dangerous dog encounters, or to inform me that I was trespassing on private property. Neither were there any for Sara. When I did come upon the four dogs that attacked me, none of them were physically restrained. Neither were the three dogs that attacked Sara. Bo knew his dogs were dangerous, but he still allowed his dogs unhindered access to the lobby of his business a few minutes before his customer was due to arrive. If the people in the shacks were the owners of my attackers, they also knew they owned dangerous dogs, because the attack I received from them was unhesitating and too well-coordinated for it to have been the first time that it had occurred. Yet, they allowed the four dogs to have unhindered access to me. I fought my way out of my predicament, but Sara came up one stride and one second too late to escape hers. All because the zoo keepers abandoned their duties and left the cage doors that house deadly predators wide open. Preventing territorial aggression isn't difficult. We just have to remember to be good zoo keepers and close the doors.

Final words on my attack....

Some readers will undoubtedly think it was cruel of me to hit the dogs that attacked me. I, on the other hand, did what I had to do to save my life. If anyone was cruel that day, it was the owners of the dogs. After all, it was their negligence that forced me into swinging a tree branch to stay alive. If you do think I was cruel, I pray you never find yourself under the same type of attack. If you should, I pray you are able to do whatever it takes to return to those who love you.

"If you have form'd a circle to go into,
Go into it yourself, and see how you would do."

~William Blake

Chloe and Marion Montgomery

"Three-year-old children aren't supposed to die."

No, they're not, agreed Marion, but she didn't say the words out loud to her grieving son. And, when her daughter in-law had accused her earlier in the day of "killing their child," she had also agreed, but she hadn't voiced it. In fact, Marion

Montgomery hadn't said anything to anyone since she had awoken in an intensive care unit after the first of her two surgeries a week ago; not to the police who wanted to know how it happened, nor to the news reporters that wanted to know why it happened, nor to the child protection agents that wanted to know if she knew it would happen. Even the animal control officer, who stopped by to ask her if she wanted her dog to have a private cremation, was met with silence. Marion wouldn't talk to anyone.

"I know you hear me."

Marion slowly turned her attention from the ceiling in her room to her son, who was sitting on a chair next to her bed. The loss of his only child had been hard on him. His eyes were bloodshot, with dark circles, and the wrinkles in the corner of his mouth that had always made his smile seem twice as big as it really was had become jagged on their edges, making him now look like a sad version of a scarecrow instead. New tears were running down his already-stained cheeks as he fidgeted with a button on his shirt between glances at her. Marion wanted so desperately to reach out and hold him like she had done when he was a young boy, and tell him how sorry she was. But instead, she just closed her eyes.

"Why won't you tell me what happened?" he pleaded.

In the dark place that had become Marion's self-imposed Hell, the scene of her granddaughter's head being crushed by the pressure of the dog's jaws as he shakes her like a rag doll mocks her like a merciless, evil jester that persists on repeating his agonizing joke. Acting like an unquenchable demon dancing on the stage of her sanity, the cruel jester repeats the scene over and over again until he obliterates every hidden recess that protects her precious faith. And then, in his twisted finale, he sends the dog charging at her with the bloody child still clamped in its jaws and waits for the scream that erupts from Marion's Godless body. When it comes, the jester bows, and his unpitying laughter is all that is heard.

Marion reached for her son until she could feel him grasp her bandaged hand in his. For a moment, she squeezed his hand as hard as she was able, while he gently squeezed back. Then, as the first tears since the death of her granddaughter trickled from underneath her closed eyelids, she whispered, "Because I love you too much," and then she pulled her hand away. For Marion, her private Hell held no room for anyone but her.

It was long after her son had left, and the attending nurses had dimmed the lights in her room, that Marion finally opened her eyes and reached for the Bible that she kept tucked underneath her blanket. Her neighbor and best friend had brought it, along with some peanut butter cookies she'd made, to the hospital after she had fetched it from Marion's home. The Bible and the cookies were a nice gesture, but Marion hadn't failed to notice that her best friend hadn't brought them to her room. Instead, she'd left them at the nurses' station, where they were added to the other gifts that had been dropped off by other friends who also hadn't come to see Marion. "Can you blame them?" Marion asked herself as she opened her Bible to Mark 9:36-37 and read, "He took a little child whom he placed among them. Taking the child in his arms, he said to them, "Whoever welcomes one of these little children in my name welcomes me, and whoever welcomes me does not welcome me but the one who sent me." She could still remember when she had sewn the two verses on the quilt she'd made for Chloe and how much the little girl with a smile twice as big as her daddy's had loved it. Even though she had been too young to read the stitched words, her granddaughter had delighted in the varying colors she had chosen to use and the two orange and yellow flowers that adorned each end of the scriptures. "Thank you, Nana!" her granddaughter had shouted while she hugged Marion and the new quilt at the same time. Then she had asked, "Will you watch my blanket when I'm not here?" As Marion thought back on what her answer had been at the time, she closed her Bible and started to cry. "Of course, I will. I will watch over it and protect it, and I will always do the same for you."

Sometime later, Marion fell asleep. She had fought it as long as she could because she was terrified of the nightmares that gripped her, but sleep finally took over and carried her away. At first, the dream was kind. It eased her troubled mind with the fruity smell of Jell-O as she mixed it in a bowl while Chloe kept asking if it was ready. After that, the dream put Chloe on her lap as Marion ran a brush through her granddaughter's long, red hair. Occasionally, the brush would get stuck on a tangle and Chloe would yelp in pain and ask to get down, but the promise of more Jell-O always earned Marion a few more strokes of the brush. Then, the dream took Marion to a time when she had laughed hysterically because Chloe had managed to connect the dots between her screams and the promise of more dessert from her grandmother, and had started to fake them to get the Jell-O. Eventually, the dream took her to a beautiful park, and her granddaughter was swinging and laughing, and prodding Marion to push her harder so she could go higher. Even in her dream, Marion could still feel the uneasiness that had always accompanied her whenever Chloe was swinging. The darn child had been a daredevil in a three-foot tall body, and her desire to go higher and higher in the swing had scared Marion to death. The dream was kind, and continued its parade of the cheerful and joyous times the two had shared, until the wicked jester had enough of the dream's kindness and placed Chloe back on her grandmother's lap, but this time, with a slice of American cheese held precariously by the child above the head of her grandmother's new dog.

"It's okay! It's okay! Mrs. Montgomery, wake up!"

The words of the nurse couldn't reach Marion, who was still trapped in her nightmarish memories. She gasped for air as she struggled with all of her might to get the dog off of her, but she couldn't move because she was pinned between her sofa and an old wooden chest that served as her coffee table. She tried kneeing the dog in an attempt to buck it off of her, but the same sofa and chest that had her pinned supported the dog's ability to counter the thrust of her knees. "HELP ME! HELP ME!" Marion's agonizing screams were drowned out by the roar of the dog as it tore into the arm she was using to shield her face and her throat. Blood and pieces of her arm splattered in her eyes and into her open mouth, temporarily blinding her and choking her at the same time. Marion pummeled the dog with her free arm as her body spasmed and her throat constricted, but within seconds, she could feel herself losing consciousness. At that moment, the same adrenaline that has saved both the hunter and the hunted for thousands of years surged through Marion's veins and with its help, she was able to arch her back and throw the dog off balance enough to roll to her side. Then, with another superhuman effort, Marion ripped her arm from the dog's crushing bite and twisted her torso until she was fully on her stomach. Instantly, Marion puked, and her vomit added to the carnage she was lying in, but she could breathe.

"Wake up, Mrs. Montgomery!"

Marion could feel the dog's claws pulverizing the skin on her back, as it sunk its teeth deep into her flesh and pulled at the ribs and the ligaments below her left shoulder blade. With each jerk, the dog's powerful neck lifted Marion's body a few inches off the floor and then slammed it back down. It was after the second slam, when Marion felt her nose shatter, that she wanted to give up. But, there is no force greater than the one that is used by a mother to protect her child, and Marion had always felt like Chloe was one of her own. So, when she felt the dog's grip suddenly loosen after one of the ligaments finally ruptured in her back, she grabbed the blood-stained carpet in front of her with her one remaining good arm and began to crawl to her granddaughter.

"You're having a nightmare!"

Lying a few feet ahead of Marion was a lifeless, misshapen body that no longer resembled the little girl that had bounced onto her lap less than a minute prior. Like Marion, Chloe was lying on her stomach, but her mangled head had been wrenched so violently, her glazed eyes were staring at the ceiling instead of the floor. To Marion's horror, it was like looking at a doll that someone had taken the head off of and then put back on facing the wrong direction. "PLEASE NO! GOD HELP ME!" Marion wailed as she dragged herself across the floor. In addition to her broken neck, most of the red hair that used to shine like new copper had been yanked from Chloe's scalp and now lay scattered over the floor in mounds of chaotic fiber and gore. Marion had always adored Chloe's hair and despised her mother for constantly making pigtails or fancy braids out of it. As a result, each morning, after Chloe was dropped off by her mother on her way to work, Marion's first order of business was restoring the beautiful scarlet locks to their unhindered splendor. As she crawled, Marion carefully gathered up all of the damaged strands she could reach. Even while she endured an unfathomable terror, she was determined to save Chloe's hair and render its beauty once again.

"Wake up!

Marion froze. A large shadow, acting like a damp fog rising from the dark surface of a lake, slowly inched its way up her body until it stopped above her outstretched hand. The dog had not continued its aggression after Marion had started crawling away, but now she could sense its presence standing over her. As Marion lay motionless, she felt the dog's hot saliva dripping on the back of her head and knew the searing pain of the dog's teeth tearing into her body would come any second. Closing her eyes, she prayed for a quick death and braced herself, but the attack never happened. Instead, the dog walked over to Chloe's body and began pushing it with its nose. Marion, fearing the dog was about to start feeding on her granddaughter, screamed and pulled at the carpet in a desperate attempt to reach Chloe and the dog. The dog initially turned in her direction as she crawled toward it, but, after a moment, it discarded her with an uncaring glance and turned its attention back to the dead child. Several shoves later with its enormous muzzle, Marion watched as the dog snatched up a half-eaten slice of American cheese from where Chloe had been lying and swallow it.

"You gave us quite the scare last night. Yes, ma'am, you did!"

Marion smiled at the nurse as she watched her unwrap the bandage on her arm. She was always the first person to greet Marion when she woke up, and her soft voice and genuine friendliness brought a much-needed comfort after a night filled with terror. Marion knew she had volunteered to work each night so she could watch over her while she slept. The nurse hadn't told her so, but Marion had spent enough time in hospitals, watching her husband slowly rot away from the cancer he'd gotten from Agent Orange, to know their standard work schedule. Now, as she gazed at the nurse delicately removing the last part of the bandage, she was ashamed of her self-pity and the fact that she had never expressed her gratitude to the nurse. Embarrassed, she turned and looked away.

"There's no need to feel ashamed about what happened to your granddaughter, Mrs. Montgomery. Sometimes, bad things happen, but they're all part of God's plan."

"God's plan?" Marion questioned silently, and then her embarrassment quickly turned to anger. Reaching under her blanket, she grabbed the Bible her husband had carried with him on the sixty-four missions he'd flown over northern Vietnam, and hurled it across the room. *What plan of God's would include using a dog to kill an innocent, three-year old child?* Marion wondered. As she lay in her bed and fumed, Marion recalled the heated argument she'd had with her son and his wife after she had introduced them to her new dog. Both had been very angry with Marion for adopting such a large dog, especially while Chloe was still so young and in her care five days a week. Even though she had tried to convince them that the dog was not a danger to Chloe, and that she would love having a pet, they'd remained adamant about Marion sending the dog back to the animal shelter from which she had adopted it. "I should have listened to them," she agonized. Then Marion remembered how the dog had always growled at her whenever she approached it while it was eating. At first, the growling alarmed her, but she figured the dog's behavior was a consequence of almost starving to death when it was homeless and running loose on the streets. Therefore, she'd forgiven the dog's aggressiveness and avoided going anywhere near it while it ate. "I guess I should have listened to the dog too," Marion admitted to herself. Finally, she forced herself to think about the moment the slice of American cheese had fallen out of Chloe's hand and how Chloe had toppled out of her lap when she'd tried to catch it. It had all happened so fast to Marion. Staring at the Bible lying on the floor across the room, the speed in which the tragedy occurred made her think about the last verse she had shared with her husband before he had died, "Man is like a mere breath; His days are like a passing shadow." Marion realized that in the time it had taken for her to inhale a single breath, Chloe had landed on top of the large dog lying on the floor between the sofa and the wooden chest a split second after the slice of cheese. In the time it had taken for Marion to exhale the breath, the dog had attacked Chloe, and then Marion was attacking the dog. By the time her breath dissipated in the air, Chloe had lost her life, and Marion was fighting to save hers.

"I know you're angry and you're questioning things, but, you should be dead right now. Therefore, the good Lord saved you for a reason. Perhaps, you should ask why He did that and not question why your granddaughter died? Besides, you don't need to worry about her. She's flying in Heaven right now!"

Ever so slowly, Marion raised her head and stared at the nurse. After a few moments, she asked, "Do you believe that?"

"Well, look who can talk after all! Yes ma'am, Mrs. Montgomery, I do believe that!"

Marion searched the nurse's face for any hint of insincerity, but there was none. Neither was there any judgment. Instead, all Marion could see was love. "Thank you," she whispered.

"No need to ever thank me."

As Marion watched, the nurse walked over to the Bible lying on the floor and carefully picked it up. After dusting it off, she returned and laid it at the foot of the bed. Then, smiling the warmest smile Marion had ever seen, she bent down and kissed her on her forehead.

"You know, my husband was also a pilot."

Marion was astonished. Only a handful of people knew of her husband, and only she knew the Bible had belonged to him. But, before she could ask the nurse how she knew, the nurse smiled again and walked out of the room.

Marion lay in her bed, contemplating what the nurse had said about Chloe flying in Heaven for most of the day, and it made her wonder if she would meet her husband, who, besides his feelings for Marion, loved flying more than anything else. "I can just imagine her begging him to let her go higher!" She chuckled. The thought of Chloe zipping through puffy white clouds and soaring over mountain streams with her late husband pushing her made Marion happy, and it brought her a deep and soothing peace that she hadn't felt since the attack. Outside, a soft rain was falling, and as Marion listened to the soothing patter of water droplets dancing on her window, she drifted off to sleep. A little while later, the rain stopped, allowing the sun's final light of the day to push through the narrow gap left by Marion's partially-closed curtains. As the evening progressed, the light slowly crept across the room until it came to settle on the foot of Marion's bed, resting on top of a worn, leather Bible with two tiny, orange and yellow flowers.

The soft heat of the sun's rays tickled Marion's cheeks as she weaved her way through a collage of orange and yellow flowers that blanketed the forest landscape. As she walked, she would glide her hands over the flowers like two small airplanes, and occasionally, she would fly the planes low enough to feel the velvet petals brush against her palms. *"Your hair matches the orange ones."* Marion smiled as she glanced over her shoulder at the dashing young man following her. He seemed out of place in his dark blue uniform with all the shiny silver buttons and creased lines, but Marion didn't care. She only had a few more days to spend with him before he left for Vietnam, so no place was out of place with him in it. "And these match yours!" Marion giggled as the plane flying on her right side swooped down and plucked one of the brilliant yellow flowers. *"Not a bad maneuver. You would make a great wing man."* The plane that held the yellow flower suddenly banked hard to the left and reversed its course. While Lieutenant Montgomery watched, the plane flew directly at him and at the last possible moment gained altitude, circled behind his neck, and landed on his shoulder. "You mean, wing 'woman'," Marion crooned, and then she kissed him while winking at the three-year old girl with orange hair nestled in his arms. The dream was kind.

Self Defense Aggression - Swing Hard or Die

Some time ago, I was discussing self-defense aggression with another behaviorist when she asked, "Isn't all dog aggression defensive by nature? Meaning, whether aggression is used in defense of a bone, a territory, or oneself, it's still defensive aggression, correct?" I thought it was an excellent question, but I could sense it was more of a preface than a question, so I encouraged her to proceed before I answered. "If I am correct, shouldn't all aggression just be labeled as defensive, instead of making things complicated by labeling it as competitive, territorial, and self-defense"?

I have always been a huge fan of keeping it simple. When I was a boy in Fairbanks, Alaska, survival was always about simplicity. Build a fire, or freeze. Know where you're going, or become hopelessly lost. When you meet wolves and bears, leave them alone. Making it hard made it hard to stay alive, so simplicity was the rule of the day.

However, I answered no because, as you have read up to this point, the "Hammer" is a versatile tool that serves the many needs of wolves, who in turn passed it, along with many of the same needs, to our dogs. Therefore, canine aggression won't allow itself to be neatly packaged underneath one label. If it did, many of its goals would never be met. For instance, the goal to acquire food would require an offensive aggression from a wolf to kill prey, then a defensive aggression (competitive aggression) to keep its food from other wolves, or interspecific competitors, should the need arise. Toss a bone to three dogs who place the same high value on it, and one of them will have to use an offensive aggression to gain control of it (competitive aggression), then possibly a defensive aggression (also, competitive aggression) to keep it from one, or both of the other dogs. Notice in the latter scenario, involving dogs that did not need to kill the bone, the aggression that would have been required of the dog who ended up with it, would have required an offensive and a defensive approach, just like in the former scenario involving the wolf. In both, the wolf and the dog would have had to shift their aggression from one to the other to obtain their goal and keep their prize.

Thus, aggression cannot simply be confined to the requirements of one purpose, or "label." It has to have the ability to be both offensive and defensive, and shift from one to the other when needed. It must also be given the capacity to control or to kill. And, in cases such as what occurred to Marion and Chloe Montgomery, it has to be able to do them all within a few seconds.

The dog Marion Montgomery adopted from the Animal Shelter was a massive, powerfully-built animal that had already demonstrated to Marion more than a few times that it considered food to be a very high-value commodity, and that it would attack her if necessary to keep it for itself. Therefore, it doesn't come as a surprise that when Chloe landed on top of the dog while it was trying to eat the cheese that she had dropped on the floor a split second before, the dog attacked her. Again, because dogs are not part of the human race and do not possess human cognition and all that comes with it (i.e., morality, counterfactual conditioning, theory of mind, language, and a capacity for tool making), their behavior will always be governed by the natural mechanisms that manipulate it. Consequently, the dog did not take into consideration that it was only a harmless, three-year old child that was landing on top of its head. Instead, Chloe was perceived by the dog as an attacking competitor, willing to wage physical combat for the cheese. The dog, sensing this, immediately evoked the evolutionary rule of "MINE", and counter-attacked by snatching Chloe's head and shaking her until her neck broke. Then, with no more consideration than he would have given to a dead cat, he discarded his competitor by tossing Chloe's body several feet away.

In the three seconds it took for that to happen, Marion was already throwing herself on the dog in an attempt to save her granddaughter. The dog, suddenly finding itself unable to escape from an attack from a much larger, fist-pounding assailant, switched its aggression from competitive to self-defense. As an elderly woman, Marion was no match for the dog, who thrashed her with a ferocity usually reserved for a kill-or-be-killed situation, until she signified that she had been defeated and was no longer a threat to the dog by crawling away. The entire incident lasted less than thirty seconds and, during that time, the dog employed both competitive and self-defense aggression to kill a competitor and conquer an attacker. Afterwards, the dog searched for the slice of cheese that had gotten stuck to Chloe's body while she was being killed and, upon finding it, it ate it and went about life as though nothing had occurred.

Unfortunately, this very abrupt shift in canine aggression from competitive (or territorial) to violent self-defense aggression is a common occurrence among humans that get physical with dogs in ways that are interpreted as a threat by dogs, and thousands of people are seriously injured each year as a result. This shift to self-defense aggression directed toward humans is most often seen when people try a "hands on the dog" approach to:

- breaking up fights that are occurring between dogs for either competitive or territorial reasons
- stopping dog attacks to themselves, or to other people
- taking something from dogs that they don't want them to have
- punishing dogs

In their minds, people who do this believe that their "hands on the dog" approach will be received by the dog as their way of preventing them from being harmed, or from harming someone else, or from committing harmful behaviors that could cause them to eventually be re-homed, or euthanized. However, the interpretation of the intent of ANY physical interaction with a dog is left up to the dog, and sometimes, the dog perceives it as a bodily threat while the person touching the dog does not. If a dog should ever perceive the physical interaction of a human as a threat, regardless of how it is intended, it will use self-defense aggression and elevate it to whatever level is necessary for it to survive the encounter. And it will continue with its fierce aggression until one of three conditions emerges: its adversary is defeated, it is defeated, or the opportunity to escape its adversary becomes available.

The attack to William Monroe by his Pit Bull, Cooper, was initiated by competitive aggression when the dog perceived William's attempt to take the bone he was chewing on as a direct challenge to him for the bone. However, when he attacked William to drive him away from the bone, William panicked and attacked back; not because he wanted to teach Cooper a lesson, or to defeat him so he could take the bone, but because he was under siege from a dangerous animal and feared for his life. Nevertheless, Cooper didn't see it that way. Instead, he interpreted William's "hands on the dog" approach to saving his own life as his intent to inflict great harm or death to him, much in the same way as the dog that fought Marion. As a result, Cooper instantly shifted his aggression from competitive to self-defense, employed the same level of ferociousness as the other dog, and mauled William until he no longer posed a danger to him. Then, like the other dog, which turned its attention back to the cheese after defending itself from Marion, Cooper turned his attention back to the bone after killing William.

Every victim that I have interviewed that was involved in a sudden shift in canine aggression from competitive, or territorial, to self-defense, was devastated by the incident. None of them could believe how savage and uncontrollable the dog had become after they had made physical contact with it, and, fearing death, or serious injury from the dog, they had all fought back. Consequently, the dog they fought escalated its aggression and continued its attack because it feared death, or serious injury from them as well. In every case, the battle endured until one of the combatants no longer felt threatened by the other combatant. If you were able to rewind the tape of the attacks to Chloe and Marion Montgomery, and William Monroe, you would see the same thing.

However, if you could edit the tape and substitute their actions with ones that would not have been threatening to the dogs involved, or if you could make them stop fighting sooner, the dogs' use of aggression and the subsequent outcomes of the tragedies would drastically change. For example, if Chloe had fallen on the floor, either in front of or behind the dog, instead of landing on top of it, the dog would have likely used competitive aggression in a purely defensive form instead of offensive. In other words, had that happened, Chloe would have received just a growl, or a bite sufficient enough to keep her away from the cheese instead of a full-on attack. As a result, her **worst** day would have been possibly a few stitches instead of a broken neck. Regarding Marion, no one can blame her actions. Drastic times do indeed call for drastic measures, and I am not sure if I have yet to meet the parent, or grandparent that wouldn't have done the same thing as her under the same circumstances, especially if it involved a dog attacking a child. The same goes for William and his actions or anyone else, for that matter, that finds themselves fighting for their lives after being attacked by a deadly animal. Nevertheless, Marion almost ended up being buried next to her granddaughter, and William *was* buried, because their actions were interpreted by each of their dogs as those of someone intent on harming them, which resulted in the dogs escalating their aggression to a level much higher than what had been needed to vanquish a three-year old competitor (in Chloe and Marion's case), or to keep a bone (in William's).

However, at the moments during their struggles when Marion and William were on their backs and realized THEY were the ones fighting for their lives and not the other way around, had they found the ability to stop fighting back right then, both dogs would have ceased their attack, just like one of them did when Marion started crawling away. Consequently, Marion would not have received the injuries that almost killed her, and William would, most likely, be alive today.

In the attacks that occurred to Marion and William, each dog had a goal. Because all aggression is dangerous to both the antagonist and the recipient, there must be a valid reason to use it and an end goal that makes an effort worth the risk. Competitive aggression acquires and defends high-value food and objects, and territorial aggression gains and protects high-value property, as their goals. Self-defense aggression eliminates threats by forcing them to surrender, or it creates the ability to escape from them. In accomplishing the goal of any of the three, physical contact by the dog is not always required, thus lessening some of the risks. Sometimes, a dog can keep its owner's new shoe just by growling or showing its teeth at its owner, instead of biting him. Dogs run off perceived trespassers, such as delivery people, all the time by lunging at the front door, or barking their heads off, and many needle-wielding veterinarians have been backed into the corner of their exam rooms by dogs that had become savvy to the pain their needle inflicts. On the flip side, for aggression to be evoked, regardless of the risk of its use, it doesn't always require the competitor, trespasser, or threat to make physical contact with the dog. In the cases of Earl May, William Monroe, and Sara McAlister, none of them physically provoked the dogs that killed them. Earl was simply walking down a dirt road when he was attacked, William had only moved a foot off of the refrigerator he was leaning up against in his kitchen, and Sara had just opened the door to a repair shop lobby. Still, all of the dogs attacked, and the goal of each was obtained.

Even though Marion Montgomery, unlike the others, did physically provoke her attacker into utilizing self-defense aggression against her, of the three types of aggression, self-defense has become much more reactive and far less predictable in today's dogs than the other two. So much so, that it now actually requires the least amount of physical provocation to be elicited, and attacks by dogs utilizing self-defense aggression to obtain their goal of eliminating threats to them are occurring to more and more people who never touched the dog that bit them, or did anything that they thought was the least bit antagonistic. This is happening because nowadays, a threat can take the form of almost anything, including all races, ages, and genders of humans, as well as their accompanying body language, as actions threatening enough to warrant an attack by a dog. These actions encompass a wide variety of everyday, non-hostile gestures or changes in body position, which range from people raising their hands above their heads to extending a hand toward a dog to pet it, or even offering a treat. Case in point: I have fed many nervous dogs treats with my feeding hand facing palm up with never a problem. However, the instant I turned my feeding hand palm down, as though I were going to pet them, some of them attacked me. For those that tried to bite me, all it took was a simple turning of my hand that held treats to a different position to pose a substantial enough threat for them to respond aggressively toward me. More than likely, their reaction was the byproduct of having been swatted on their muzzles by humans that had hit them with an open hand facing palm down, and even though that wasn't my intent when I turned my hand palm down, they took it that way. Fortunately, after I was bitten a few times, I learned to keep my hand palm up when feeding treats to nervous dogs. Other examples of typical human body language that cause some dogs to feel threatened enough to bite include people who stand up quickly from a seated position, causing their profile to nearly double in size, thus increasing their threat to a nearby dog, individuals who approach too closely to dogs that are fearful of them and can't escape, or strangers that bend over unfamiliar dogs to pet them. Unless you are very familiar with the dog, I wouldn't recommend that you do the latter, because bending your torso so that it looms over an unfamiliar dog is a risky proposition at best. Imagine a strange person, four times your size, bending over you. Unless you were clear that their intent was not to harm you, you'd probably be a bit concerned. The problem is, dogs often express their concern in such cases with their teeth, whereas you would most likely start off by politely asking the stranger to move back a little before you bit them.

The reasons for the growing development of a paranoia-like use of self-defense aggression among domestic dogs lie with several factors:

- The inability to discern valid threats
- Restricted use of alternate defensive mechanisms
- An overall weakening genetic baseline

The inability of dogs to distinguish legitimate human threats is blamed entirely on a lack of socialization by many experts. That's interesting, but it's incorrect in its conclusion for a few reasons. First, socialization is defined as "the process of internalizing the norms and ideology of society."[21] Therefore, blaming a lack of internalization of normal human behavior and beliefs for dog attacks would be okay if dogs were human and were even remotely capable of such. However, they aren't and they can't. Also, people don't always act "normal" themselves, so what is the norm? Millions of humans have not only taught dogs over the years that their behavior is different than theirs, but it is also incredibly inconsistent, and it is often harmful. My previous example of the interpretation of a palm up versus palm down hand position by some dogs helps to explain this. Millions of dogs have been lovingly stroked by the palms of human hands, while some have been struck by them, and a lot of them have received both love and an attack from the very same hand. Another example occurs with obedience training. Some dogs are trained to return to their owners when they are called and are given a reward when they obey. Then the next time they're called and they return, the owner of the dog replaces the typical reward for obeying with a swift kick in their butt for having left the yard in the first place!

Dogs thrive on the familiar, not the unfamiliar; so much so that if writer and philosopher Apuleius had been writing about dogs instead of demons in his work titled "De Deo Socratis" (On the God of Socrates), he would have surely written that familiarity breeds content, instead of contempt. Regrettably, human behavior isn't always familiar with dogs, and no matter how much time dogs spend socializing with them, the only consistent thing they can expect is inconsistency. Therein lies the real problem. The threshold of what dogs presume to be real danger in their human-filled eco-niche has lowered considerably over the years due to inconsistent human behavior, not a lack thereof. As a result, some dogs have adopted the policy of shooting first and asking questions later when they have any doubts at all as to which human behavior is threatening to them and which isn't.

Attacks by dogs because of their restricted use of alternate defensive mechanisms is another problem that has arisen from their adaptation to living with humans that live in close quarters with other humans. Today, with 62.7% of the U.S. population currently residing in urban cities where leash laws are enforced and living space is limited,$_{22}$ dogs have become nearly powerless to flee perceived danger. These city-dwelling dogs often find themselves on a leash connected to their owners, or in a confined space such as a cage, vehicle, alleyway, or small apartment, leaving them with only the ability to attack should they feel threatened by another person.

Lastly, regarding a weakening genetic baseline, mankind has manipulated wolf genes for so long, and so often, in his attempt to achieve a perfect state of tameness in today's domestic wolf, that he's overdone it. As a result, more and more dogs are being born so far beyond tame that they're fearful of mankind. By the time many of these types of dogs reach the tender age of one year old, they're utilizing self-defense aggression against anyone and everyone, because everything represents an imaginary threat to its safety. It's sad, but it's true. Dogs are becoming confused, confined, and corrupted by mankind, and as a consequence of their seemingly "unprovoked" attacks, they are also being condemned to die.

Self-defense aggression has become a quirky beast, to say the least. Sometimes, it appears to come out of nowhere, and that's because from our viewpoint, it does. But, unlike any other form of aggression, self-defense aggression is only driven by fear for one's safety, imaginary, or not. It can attach itself to other types of aggression, or it can stand on its own, but whether it is used by a human or a dog, it must have the presence of a perceived threat to provoke it enough to stir it from its slumber. When aroused, its goal is not to acquire food or objects, or to defend property, but only to keep the human or the dog resorting to it alive. In doing so, it remains laser-focused in its aim and intensely violent in its application. It is the "Hammer" that is wielded when the bullets run out, and the long-distance attack suddenly becomes close and personal. For that reason, when nature created it, she sent instructions for its use: swing hard, or die.

Preventing Self-Defense Aggression

In 1799, in his letter to John Trumbull, George Washington wrote, *"Make them believe, that offensive operations, often times, are the surest, if not the only (in some cases) means of defense."*[23] When it comes to dogs defending themselves from perceived attacks, they heed George Washington's counsel. And when they do, their offensive operations aren't prone to persuasive speeches or acts of civil diplomacy, like many of his opponents. Instead, they're more comfortable with sheer brutality, which they use with an unrelenting determination to outlast the other guy. If the other guy at the end of their muzzle happens to be someone trying to stay alive, they'll do the same thing. They'll also bring to bear all of the brutality they can muster, and stay in the fight for as long as they can. With competitive aggression and territorial defense, the fight ends the second the high-value food, object, or territory is secure. However, with self-defense aggression, the epic battle between perceived killers, especially if it involves a large, dangerous dog, swings back and forth until one or the other is defeated, or able to escape. Therefore, even though competitive or territorial aggression <u>initiates</u> most of the fatal dog attacks to humans, it is self-defense aggression that usually <u>finishes</u> them. That's why preventing self-defense aggression is so important; once you're in it, you may not get out of it.

Preventing competitive or territorial aggression is more difficult than preventing self-defense aggression because of the infinite number of possible igniters involved in the two, as discussed in their respective chapters. However, with self-defense aggression, there is only one possible igniter: the presence of a threat to the dog. This makes preventing it relatively easy if the following advice is heeded and put into action:

Don't Screw Up!

If you ever find yourself dealing with self-defense aggression, it's likely because you screwed up by not doing a good job keeping yourself from being attacked when you were confronted with competitive aggression, or someone else screwed up by not being a good zoo keeper and you're now having to deal with their dog. Therefore, don't screw up! There's a reason why this chapter is sitting where it is in this book. Read and heed what I wrote in the chapters concerning competitive and territorial defense. It'll keep you and others out of the line of fire of self-defense aggression.

Don't Force the Issue.

In the human-to-dog scheme, it's not dogs that initiate self-defense aggression, it's the humans. We force the issue by starting the fight, or not saying "uncle" and fighting back (like William Monroe). In the case of Marion Montgomery, she did both. Other times, we force the issue, either intentionally or unintentionally, by getting too close to dogs that aren't able to escape our approach. When we do, we are immediately attacked by the dog. Here's why:

Surrounding all dogs and wolves (even humans) are two imaginary zones, one residing inside the other. Unlike a dog's territory and its "invincible center," which are both stationary zones, these zones constantly surround dogs and wolves, and accompany them wherever they go.

The outer zone, which I call the *threat* zone, serves the purpose of assisting a dog or a wolf in avoiding detection by a possible threat, or as a long-distance warning to the threat of its intent to attack if the threat comes too close. The threat zone expands and contracts as dogs and wolves move from wide-open areas to areas that more densely forested, or, in the case of dogs, where their view is more restricted by man-made structures. In either case, the threat zone typically stretches to the furthest distance that a dog or a wolf can see. When wolves spot another predator at a distance, such as another wolf or a large bear, they will immediately freeze. By not moving, they are often able to avoid detection while they work through the process of identifying the other predator as a possible friend or foe. Freezing works because the eyes of most predators are dominated by a higher ratio of rods than cones in the iris, which optimizes their ability to detect movement, especially in low light. The wolf inherently knows this, and will remain immobile in an attempt to avoid detection by the other predator until the identification process is complete.

Once the identification process has been completed and the other predator is determined to be a foe, rather than a friend, the wolf will run the possible foe through a threat matrix, where it will quickly determine the severity of the threat that it poses. If the threat level is determined to be high, the wolf may elect to get a head start on escaping by fleeing while its foe is still at a distance. In cases where escape is not possible, or if the wolf is defending a recent kill, it may elect to hold its ground and hope that it is not discovered by the other predator. In the event that it is discovered, however, the wolf will switch its behavior from immobility to visual deterrence by making itself look like a worthy opponent to its foe. In doing so, its hackles will reflexively rise along its spine. Its tail will shoot straight up and its chest will puff out until both are twice as big as normal. Its stance will widen and its body will become rigid, while its lips pull back to expose its fangs. Lastly, its eyes will narrow and its stare will send a silent but ominous message across the gulf separating the two- STAY AWAY, or ELSE!

In about half of the cases I have observed, the other predator, after watching the wolf's visual display of deterrence and running the wolf through its own threat matrix, will move closer to get a better look at things, regardless of the show. Most often, this is because the other predator knows that if the wolf hasn't hightailed it out of the area, then there is more than likely a good reason for the show. Either the wolf is protecting food, or it is a much inferior predator trying to bluff its way out of a tight spot. If the other predator happens to be an alien wolf, it may seize the opportunity to eliminate an inferior competitor and possibly get something to eat at the same time. Nevertheless, as soon as the blustering wolf detects any forward movement by the other predator, it will instantly supplement its visual deterrence with a vicious auditory warning. In other words, "I just showed you how fierce I am. NOW, LET ME TELL YOU ABOUT IT!"

Alas, if the wolf's vicious auditory warning falls on deaf ears because the other predator isn't convinced enough by it, or the visual show, to stay away, the other predator will continue its advance until it crosses the threshold of the wolf's *critical* zone. When this happens, it's time for the wolf to walk the talk (attack), or run while it still can (escape). If the wolf is defending a recent kill, but still perceives the closing predator as a severe threat, it will not risk attacking the other predator to keep its food. Instead, it will flee and abandon its meal. But, if it can't flee for some reason, it will evoke self-defense aggression, use offense as a good defense, and make the first strike. When it does, it will throw its entire life into its attack by utilizing every ounce of strength, toughness, and knowledge it has gained from surviving in the wild up to that point. And it will keep bringing all of it until its foe is defeated, or the defending wolf dies. There is no violence that can match the violence used to stay alive, and the arena where the battle of kill-or-be-killed is always fought is the critical zone: the most coveted and protected zone of all.

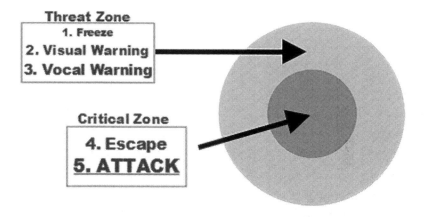

Threat Zone
1. Freeze
2. Visual Warning
3. Vocal Warning

Critical Zone
4. Escape
5. ATTACK

As you approach dogs, especially ones you are not familiar with, always keep the threat and critical zones in mind and watch the dog closely. This goes for whether you are approaching a dog that is in a home, a yard, or a vehicle, or is being walked by its owner on a leash. It also applies to whether the dog has something in its possession or not. If you are perceived as a possible threat or competitor by the dog you are approaching, it will momentarily freeze, or become stiffer in its movement if it is being walked, and then promptly shift to displaying behaviors that are either fearful or aggressive as you close the distance. If it does, stop your advance immediately if the dog is not being walked, or create more space by giving the dog a wide berth if it is, because you have just entered the dog's threat zone. After you stop, or while you pass by, avoid the temptation to stare at the dog even if it's staring at you. Staring back communicates a possible intent to attack on your part, which affirms the dog's suspicion as to whether you are a threat, and consequently, you could be attacked by the dog prematurely. However, while standing still, or passing by a moving dog, continue to observe the dog with your peripheral vision. If the dog is in possession of something, it may consider your approach as a threat to the food or object that it has. If the dog doesn't have anything, then its behavior indicates that it considers you as the threat, and you are now dealing with self-defense aggression and not competitive aggression. If this is the case, most dogs not being walked will display characteristics of fearful behavior such as shaking, ears pinned back against their head, tail tucked, tongue-flicking, yawning, excessive panting, and, don't forget, tail-wagging - the ever-persistent bait. You may also observe the dog taking quick glances out of the corner of its eyes. If so, it's looking for an escape route. If it doesn't have one, you will need to slowly back away from the dog so as not to inadvertently enter its critical zone, because if you do, you will certainly be attacked. Even if the dog has what looks like a suitable escape route to you, still back out of the threat zone, because the escape route may not be suitable for the dog and any further advance on your part will provoke self-defense aggression. While doing so, do not second-guess your decision and attempt to win over the dog with your charming personality, or by feeding it treats instead. Friendly, treat-bearing people are bitten all of the time for entering critical zones when they shouldn't.

If the dog is being walked, fearful behavior will most likely be replaced by aggressive behavior such as lunging, growling, barking, or snapping of the jaws while you are passing through the dog's threat zone. The cause for this substitution in behavior is the fact that threatening situations occur more quickly with moving dogs than stationary dogs, which forces the moving dog to process the approach of an unfamiliar person as friend or foe much faster. This requirement for fast processing leads to more incorrect assumptions of "foe" than it does with dogs that are given more time to assess the person advancing toward them. In other words, if a dog is forced by speed into guessing whether or not an approaching unfamiliar person is a threat, they are going to guess that they're a threat for survival reasons and treat the person as such until the threat either proves otherwise or is neutralized. While this is happening, they will instinctively become aggressive because their other option for dealing with the threat, which is to flee, has been eliminated by the leash that connects them to their owners. This aggressive behavior will be reinforced because even though the dog acts aggressively, most people pass by it and continue walking in the direction they were headed, albeit a little faster, regardless of the dog's behavior. Unfortunately, the dog interprets their lack of physical combat and subsequent walking away as fleeing on their part, and learns a valuable lesson. When threatening people approach you and you can't run because you're on a leash, act aggressively and they'll leave you alone! Success begets success, and there you have it! Whenever you encounter such a dog when walking, be sure to give plenty of space between you and the dog, because not all of you needs to pass through the dog's critical zone in order to be bitten. Any part of you, including your swinging hand, leg, or foot, is fair game if it crosses the border dividing the threat and critical zones.

Keeping the two imaginary zones, threat and critical, at the forefront of my mind whenever I meet unfamiliar dogs has saved me from being bitten more times than I can remember. Every time a dog's behavior indicates that I may have entered its threat zone, I never forced the issue by advancing further. Instead, I always immediately back out of the zone and rethink my plan for engaging the dog safely. I highly recommend you do the same.

Keep Your Hands Off!

Like the threat zone, the critical zone surrounding a dog is fluid in that it expands and contracts as a reaction to the dog's environment. At home, where a dog is familiar with its territory and the people who live in it, the critical zone will contract until it is very close to the dog's body. Conversely, if the same dog is relocated to an unfamiliar location inhabited by strange people who could be possible threats, its critical zone will significantly expand. Still, whether the dog is in a familiar or an unfamiliar setting, the moment you touch it, you will have just entered the dog's critical zone and made physical contact with the epicenter of a possible attack. Whether an attack erupts or not will depend solely upon how the dog interprets the <u>intent</u> of your physical contact. Contrary to what you may think, its subsequent response will have <u>everything</u> to do with that interpretation, and <u>nothing</u> to do with how much you love your dog, or how much you think it loves you. Granted, the vast majority of dogs do enjoy being touched by people, and they often solicit their physical contact. However, no dog is receptive to being touched when they feel threatened, regardless of their attachment to the one threatening them. Marion Montgomery had grown fond of her dog and it had enjoyed her petting many times before it tried to kill her after one occasion when it interpreted her physical contact as a threat.

The same thing occurred to William Monroe when he made the fatal mistake of "attacking" Cooper after Cooper attacked him first. For many years, I have listened to the stories of dog owners and horrified parents that told of the aftermath of when a loving embrace to the family dog suddenly erupted into an attack. Many of the emotions that humans possess accompanied their stories: shock, fright, anger, sadness, vengeance, hate, hopelessness, and so forth. They were devastated, to say the least.

At the end of the day, it all boils down to interpretation, and a dog can interpret a touch by a human fifty million different ways to Sunday, but if one of the fifty million interpretations happens to be threatening, then expect the dog to try to escape from you or attack you. And because you happen to be so close that you're actually touching the dog, if it does attack, you will be unable to avoid it. Therefore, really, really, think before you reach into the critical zone of a strange dog to pet it. If the dog is displaying the least fearful or aggressive behavior while it's in your presence, try tossing, not handing, it a treat from <u>outside</u> its threat zone. By doing so, you will probably earn its trust and friendship a lot sooner, and it'll keep you safer in the meantime. Also, give an extra second of thought as to why you've decided to physically separate dogs that are fighting when their physical composition is much more able to withstand the punishment of tooth and claw than yours. In addition, most dogs that are grabbed by screaming humans while they are engaged in fighting with another dog will interpret such physical contact as an additional attack, and will respond in the same manner as Marion Montgomery's dog and employ a counter-attack to the human that grabbed them. The vast majority of dog owners that I know who tried a "hands on the dog" approach to separating fighting dogs ended up more severely injured than either of the dogs involved in the fight. Using a broom, a hose, or anything other than yourself to break up a fight is a much wiser choice. As for you grandparents, it really is ok to tell your grandson or granddaughter not to hug or kiss your dog when they come for a visit. I know you view your grandchildren as family, but your dog may not. Consequently, a close-quarter squeeze around the neck by them may be interpreted as an attempt at strangulation by your dog, and they could be bitten in the face as a result. Finally, for those of you that insist on a kicking, grabbing, or punching approach to reprimanding dogs, expect to be bitten. If you attack a dog, it will attack you back. It's just one of nature's many instances of cause-and-effect.

These are just a few examples of when not to touch a dog, and the list goes on and on. I could fill an entire book with examples and still not cover all of the possibilities of how our contact with dogs can misrepresent our actual intentions. On account of this, whenever there is any doubt as to how your physical contact may be interpreted by your dog or a strange dog, <u>don't touch it</u>. It is important to keep in mind that any contact that is perceived as a threat by the dog, whether you intend it or not, will serve as a flashpoint for a possible attack. So, if you must touch a fearful or aggressive dog for some reason, or the dog is about to touch you in an aggressive manner, do your best to use any method or equipment that allows you to engage the dog safely. In my opinion, the best tools for handling or avoiding aggressive or potentially aggressive dogs without having to sacrifice a part of your body include:

- your brain (that's right, the thing between your ears - best tool ever invented for preventing canine aggression
- sturdy leash and collar (both are only as good and as strong as the handler - a weak handler will easily be overpowered by a stronger dog)
- heavy-duty welder's gloves (good for grabbing small to medium dogs)

- catch poles (sometimes referred to as rabies poles - good for controlling dogs of all sizes)
- brooms with straw ends (porcupine on a stick! - good for driving small to intermediate size dogs away from you by jabbing them with it)
- thick blanket (great tool to throw on top of fighting dogs - the blanket will severely, if not totally, restrict their vision, and when they can no longer see their opponent, they'll stop fighting - however, it doesn't mean that they won't reengage once they are out from underneath the blanket, so be ready to keep throwing the blanket on top of them until they stop fighting for good)
- garden hose (another great tool for breaking up dog fights as long as you're not nice about it - spray high-velocity water directly into the dogs' faces until they stop fighting)
- bear mace (very effective against dogs charging you - most brands can fire an incapacitating spray up to 35 feet away, which is 30 feet further than most personal protection sprays - it'll drop a charging dog in its tracks and keep it down long enough for you to get safely away)
- Co2 fire extinguisher (very effective against dogs charging you - if used to break up dog fights, do your best not to spray the high-pressure gas cloud directly into the dogs' eyes - usually, just firing it off near their heads is enough to stop the fight)

Ineffective tools include:

- citronella spray (the equivalent of bringing a pocket knife to a gun fight - worthless)
- air horns (could drive a fearful dog away from you, but not very effective for breaking up dog fights -dogs pin their

ears back when fighting to keep them from being torn off by the other combatant and as a result, they aren't able to hear as well - essentially like blowing a horn at an animal wearing ear muffs)
- fly swatter (really?)
- cane/baseball bat/stick (unless you plan on swinging it like I did when I was attacked in Alabama instead of poking the dog, they're very limited in their ability to fight off aggressive dogs)

If you are a dog owner, or find yourself encountering unfamiliar dogs often, I would urge you to acquire some of the tools I've recommended so you won't ever be faced with having to make physical contact with a fearful or aggressive dog. After acquiring some of the tools, keep them handy. The one time in my life that I needed my bear mace the most, I didn't have it on me, and not having it almost got me killed in Alabama. Don't let what happened to me happen to you. Lastly, please know that no tool made by mankind will ever compensate for mankind's stupidity. Mahatma Gandhi echoed this when he said, *"speed is irrelevant if you are going in the wrong direction."* If you ignore the warning signs being given off by a dog not to touch it and you proceed with touching it anyway, then you'll want to pay particular attention to the next chapter, titled, "Under Siege - Surviving an Attack."

Demonstrate and Deactivate

Have you ever visited a foreign country where you were unable to speak the language, and you had no idea of the customs of its inhabitants? If so, did you find yourself relying more on facial expressions and gestures than talking in an effort to communicate with the people you met? While doing so, did you study them more acutely in an effort to discern what was being communicated to you, or to gather insight as to their intent? Lastly, did you make an effort to categorize any consistent patterns you learned from the many facial expressions and gestures you experienced so you would know how to react properly in the event that you experienced them again? If you did, then you have a minuscule idea of what it's like to be a dog living among humans, and how they categorize patterns of human facial expressions and gestures, just like you did, so they can respond in ways that enable them to acquire food and attention from us, but also so they can avoid or control us should we become dangerous to them.

In both instances, it is a consistent pattern of behavior that enables you to successfully communicate with foreigners and for dogs to successfully communicate and interact with us. If there had not been a consistent pattern of facial expressions and gestures on the part of the foreigners, you would have never succeeded in interpreting their behavior or intentions regardless of how many days, weeks, months or years you spent interacting with them. The same goes for dogs. They are visitors in a world they don't understand, and any lack of consistent behavior on the part of its inhabitants (humans) contributes significantly to their inability to successfully interpret human behavior or their intentions, regardless of how long they spend with them. This is why increasing socialization to humans by itself is not enough to deter attacks by dogs utilizing self-defense aggression against perceived threats. For socialization to be effective in doing so, consistent patterns of non-threatening behavior MUST be adopted and always presented by the humans they are socializing with, so that dogs learn to rely upon those behaviors as non-threatening. Otherwise, it would be like navigating through a minefield each day. Some land mines you step on will be fine because they're practice mines, while the others, the real ones, will blow up in your face. However, you won't know which is which until you step on one because no one gave you a map showing you the location of either type of mine. When dogs aren't presented with a map of a human behavioral minefield, they become fearful that every mine will blow up in their faces, and as a consequence, they rightfully overreact to the slightest feel of anything other than real dirt. After all, when it comes to guessing whether something is dangerous or not, nature taught both them and wolves that you don't often get a second chance at guessing correctly. If we want to obtain reliable, non-aggressive responses from dogs to non-threatening behaviors on our part, then we have to make sure that one of our "practice" mines never blows up in their face. Accomplishing this will require patience, emotional control, and discipline any time you interact with your dog. It will also require a two-step approach that I call demonstrate and eliminate.

Demonstrate: If we wish to teach dogs that our "everyday" normal human behaviors, including gestures, physical contact, and voice inflections, should not be construed as a threat, then we need to demonstrate to them that they aren't. The best way to accomplish this is by starting at home with a dog or puppy that you have owned long enough that it is familiar and comfortable with your behavior, and then branching out into the world when you feel your dog is ready. Start by purposely making numerous and varied physical motions near and toward your dog each day. These should be movements and gestures that your dog would be subjected to with unfamiliar human encounters (e.g. rapidly stand from a seated position, making a fast approach, holding your hand(s) above your head, waving, bending over your dog, reaching for it quickly). If a particular movement frightens your dog, try performing it at a greater distance and work your way closer while tossing an occasional treat its way. Keep this up until your dog is either no longer concerned with the movement, or has adopted a concerned, but not frightened, attitude toward it. While performing all movements and gestures, be sure to demonstrate a calm confidence to your dog, especially if it becomes frightened by any of them. By doing so, your dog will interpret your calmness and confidence as a sign that there is no danger present, and therefore, fight-or-flight mechanisms initially evoked by the movement or gesture will diminish with exposure to them.

After your dog becomes relaxed or very tolerable to your movements and gestures, start adding a variety of physical contact. Again, your physical contact, like the movements and gestures you trained your dog to accept, should mimic those that it would be subjected to with unfamiliar human encounters (e.g. pat on the head or back, stroking the head, neck, or torso, scratching behind the ears). However, NO KISSING! I'm not sure why we insist on kissing domesticated predators, especially in light of the fact that any human touch can be considered a threat by a dog, including a kiss to its muzzle, and if your kiss is ever interpreted as such, an attack is coming to your face! Still, even if you insist on kissing your dog, NEVER, EVER, ALLOW AN UNFAMILIAR MAN, WOMAN, OR CHILD (ESPECIALLY A CHILD) TO DO SO! Nothing upsets me more than when I watch irresponsible parents let their toddler walk straight up to a strange dog and kiss it, and they and the dog's owner do nothing to prevent it. If you've been one of those parents or dog owners please re-read my dedication pages and pay particular attention to all of the dead children. One bite from a medium to large size dog can crush a toddler's skull faster than you can say "good-bye."

Continue with the physical contact training, minus kissing, until your dog demonstrates that it is either receptive or actually solicits the contact. At any time during the contact training, should your dog become frightened or anxious about a particular touch, stop that particular touch immediately and try reintroducing it again at a later time with treats involved.

Finally, supplement your movements, gestures, and physical contact with a myriad of vocal sounds that would be typical of visitors to your home or strangers greeting you and your dog while on a walk. The pitch of your voice should change from high to deep and from a whisper to a shout and they should be tried with varying combinations of movements, gestures, and physical contact. While doing so, if a specific pitch or volume causes your dog to become frightened or anxious, immediately switch your voice to a volume or an inflection that your dog is more comfortable with and try reintroducing the distressing sound at a later time with treats or while playing with your dog.

Any behavior by humans conducted outside of the established "safe" pattern you have demonstrated may or may not be interpreted as a threat by dogs, but by at least pointing out which behaviors are NOT a valid threat, the incidences of dogs reacting aggressively because they assumed incorrectly will diminish.

Deactivate: Even after you have completed extensive desensitization training to normal human behaviors, your dog may occasionally misinterpret a stranger's behavior as threatening and attempt to utilize self-defense aggression against them to neutralize the threat. When this occurs, you will need to deactivate your dog's aggression by immediately taking control of the situation and by not inadvertently reinforcing its behavior. For instance, I always get a kick out of the shocked reaction of a dog owner when I tell them, "No, your dog was NOT protecting you! Rather, it was protecting itself, but because you were occupying space inside of its critical zone while it was doing so, it appeared that way!" They are always shocked, and some are even let down, because that's what they believed at the time when their dog had acted aggressively toward a stranger while it was being walked. I then go on to explain that if their dog had been leashed to a tree instead of them, it would have acted the same way under the same threatening condition. No hard feelings. However, even though I always chuckle at their facial expressions after my explanation, I eventually have to get serious and point out how their reassurance ("it's okay! It's okay!"), or their attempt to reclassify the stranger ("He's a friend!") at that moment actually acted as a reinforcer of their dog's aggressive behavior instead of what it was intended for. Their dog, while aggressively motivating a perceived human threat to move out of its threat or critical zone, was encouraged and egged on by its misguided owner. Consequently, its aggressive response was rewarded by both the actions of the perceived threat and its owner. Allow that to happen with a few more encounters with strangers, and the aggressive response will not only increase in severity, but it'll also become automatic, which is far worse. Therefore, when such conditions arise, be mindful not to reinforce your dog's behavior by petting or sweet-talking it while it is acting aggressively. Instead, immediately deactivate your dog by making it sit and be quiet while the perceived threat approaches and/or leaves the area. When your dog has done so, reward its good behavior. This will serve to not only to teach your dog that sitting and being quiet is a viable and reward-able substitute for aggression in making perceived threats go away, but it will also positively change the behavioral response of the people your dog encounters, thereby making their actions less threatening, which is important for proper friend or foe identification. When people are afraid of dogs, they act afraid. When they act afraid, they communicate fear or possible aggression to dogs. Dogs, in turn, respond with aggression or try to flee. Conversely, if you act confident and calm when in the presence of dogs, your actions tend to be less indicative of a possible attack, and dogs relax as a result. In other words, deactivation creates calmness in your dog, and this calmness brings about calmness in unfamiliar humans, which gives rise to an overall calmer interpretation of them.

Demonstrating non-threatening movements, gestures, and vocalizations to dogs, along with deactivating their aggression when it is not necessary, provides them with a map showing safe passage through a world filled with human behavioral landmines. The outcome? Less mines blowing up in everyone's face.

Overall, preventing self-defense aggression requires us to have a broader view of how our presence, our actions, and our physical contact can be interpreted as a threat by dogs. To do that, we will have to come to grips with the fact that dogs sometimes do interpret any of those as a threat to them, and attack us as a consequence. We will also have to come to grips with the fact that our reckless and ignorant behavior has given cause to their deadly interpretations. If we are to have any chance at preventing self-defense aggression by dogs, we will have to change our behavior. We will have to universally adopt and present to them consistent, non-threatening behaviors that they can come to eventually rely upon, and thus not feel the need to use aggression. Until then, we'll have to always assume that they are sometimes assuming the worst in us and not continue with behaviors that would escalate their assumption into an attack.

Under Siege - Surviving an Attack

"When you walk to the edge of all the light you have
and take that first step into the darkness of the unknown,
you must believe that one of two things will happen.
There will be something solid for you to stand
upon or you will be taught to fly."

~Patrick Overton, The Leaning Tree.

Dogs bite people. Some people are bitten for competitive, territorial defense, or self-defense reasons. Some are bitten because they acted stupidly, or someone else did. As a consequence, some people are injured, and some die. It's not a nice thought, but it's a fact of life, and it will remain so as long as people misbehave around dogs, or if they fail to properly restrain them. Whether your conduct or someone else's lack of responsibility is the reason why you've been attacked by a dog with substantial size and power, it won't matter once you are under siege. What will matter, if you wish to escape serious injury or death, is what you do next. A dog attack is a terrifying experience, but it's survivable if you follow these recommendations:

Surviving a single dog attack
Don't panic.

You're not dealing with a lunatic mad man whose behavior is unpredictable. Instead, you're dealing with an extremely predictable animal that is attacking you for the sole purpose of neutralizing a threat to its possession(s), territory, or life, and that's it. Once it accomplishes its goal, its attack to you will cease.

Lie down.

While attacking you, most large dogs will either attempt to knock you down or pull you to the ground. The reason for wanting you on the ground is two-fold. First, it lessens your ability to fight back. When wolves engage moose, caribou, or elk, they will pull them to the ground to quickly nullify the deadly effectiveness of their prey's sharp hooves, teeth, and antlers. Dogs will instinctually do the same to you. Second, dogs and wolves are four-legged predators with powerful necks and muscles spread over a <u>horizontal</u> structure designed to strike its prey or opponent like a battering ram, and then utilize a reverse thrust (like the engines of an airliner upon landing) to pull it down and then tear it apart. Because of this, it doesn't want to fight a <u>vertical</u> battle with a vertical creature (human) where it would be at a disadvantage. Instead, it wants you on the ground where it can use all of its natural abilities and you can only use a limited amount of yours. After reading that, you're probably wondering why I recommend that you do your attacker a favor and lie down voluntarily. It's exactly for that reason. You maintain control of the situation instead of being violently controlled by the dog. Trust me, if a strong, medium to large size dog has its teeth sunk into you, you're going to the ground whether you like it or not. Therefore, when you are being attacked by dogs of substantial size and power, accept the fact that you are going to the ground and limit the damage to your body by not making the dog force you down. By doing so, you will be able to take some control of your descent so as not to receive an indirect injury such as a cracked skull, broken arm, etc. by being forced to land hard, or on something harmful. And, by lying down quickly, you will avoid the devastating injuries that often accompany the thrashing and torqueing of your extremities as the dog forcibly pulls against them in its effort to get you on the ground. Go to the ground quickly. The attack is fully underway, so it's all about damage control at this point.

Curl up and cover up and don't fight back.

Once you've controlled your descent and you're on the ground, if you don't fight back, most attacks will not continue beyond this point because the goal of neutralizing its threat by the dog to its possession(s), territory, or life will have been accomplished. However, in the event that the attack continues, immediately curl up into a tight fetal position and cover your head and neck with your arms and hands. When wolves inflict fatal wounds to trespassing wolves, *"its often just one bite in the head and a skull fracture,"* according to former wildlife technician Danny Grangaard in an article published by Tim Mowry of the Fairbanks Daily News-Miner. In the article, Grangaard goes on to explain how the wounds are a result of a quick kill strategy by wolves. *"Their intention is to kill, not get in a fight,"* Grangaard explains. *"When they bite, it's some place that's going to do damage."* When dogs attack humans, their strategy is aligned with their ancestors, and they'll often try to bite the head, neck, or face of their victim to neutralize the threat without having to engage in a risky, prolonged battle. While trying to curl up and cover up, don't kick or flail at the attacking dog. If the dog has one of your arms or legs in its mouth and you can't fully curl up and cover up, that's ok, because it's not biting your head or torso at the moment. At any time, should the dog let go of your arm or leg to go for your head or neck, immediately use the arm or leg to complete the full curl up and cover up protective position and hang on tight. The attack is still underway, but stay cool, stay in control, and stay out of the fight. You may still be in damage control mode, but at least you're still alive.

Be still and suffer in silence.

If you are lying on the ground and you've managed to curl up and cover up and the dog is still attacking you, you are dealing with a very rare dog that is determined to make sure you'll never be a threat again. If you're going to survive such an attack, you will have to convince the dog you won't be by faking your death. To do that successfully, you will need to remain in your curled and covered position and be as still and as quite as you possibly can. Dead threats aren't threats any longer, but dead threats also don't move, kick, or scream. Even though you may be in a great deal of pain and you may be very scared, you will have to stay under control to survive. You will have to resist the temptation to fight back and to scream for help because doing either or both will communicate to an extremely dangerous animal that you're still alive, and if you're still alive, you're still a threat. When it realizes that, it will press harder in its attempt to kill you and it will likely succeed before help can arrive. Don't motivate it to do so. Be still. Be quiet. Be dead to the dog.

Crawl away.

After the dog finally breaks off its attack, don't attempt to stand up immediately. Standing up could fully revive the attack if the dog is nearby. Instead, while remaining in your tight fetal position, try to locate the dog. If you can't see it, listen for it. If the dog is nearby, it will be panting from exertion and you should be able to hear it. If the dog is nearby, and your injuries allow it, wait until the dog leaves the area before you attempt to get help. Should the dog not leave the area and you are in need of urgent medical care, you will have to risk another attack to get help. Still, minimize the risk by slowly crawling away in a direction that is opposite of the dog's current location. The lower and slower you move away, the less of a threat you will pose to the dog and the less likely it will re-engage you. If you have a cellphone on you and you are in a house, crawl to the closest room away from the dog and shut the door to isolate you from the dog before you make a call. While on the phone with the 911 operator, advise him or her that you have been attacked by a dog so he or she can alert the first responders before they enter your home. If you are in a house and you do not have your cellphone on you and there is no landline phone available, try to crawl to and out any door leading to the outside. If you are successful, close the door behind you quickly to trap the dog inside before you stand or scream for help.

Surviving a multi-dog attack

As if surviving a single dog attack wasn't difficult enough, in 2016, 61% of all dog bite fatalities involved more than one dog, up from a twelve-year average of 46%[24], which was already an alarmingly high percentage. This trend is very concerning because multi-dog attacks are extremely deadly and the tactic required to survive them is the polar opposite of a single -dog attack in that an offensive strategy must be employed versus a defensive one.

As I wrote in the chapter, "Zoo Keeper - Preventing Territorial Aggression," attacking an animal that is attacking you is ill-advised, but sometimes works. However, most times it doesn't, because dogs, having muscular necks, flesh-tearing fangs, and bone-crushing jaws, are much better equipped for close-quarter battle than the weaponless human they are attacking. In cases involving an attack from a single dog, not fighting back is my recommendation every day of the week. However, in cases involving two or more determined dogs, not fighting back may not be the best option in surviving because of the inherent, deadly, pack mentality that accompanies such attacks. When wolves, acting as individuals, attack other members of their pack, the mindset of the attacking wolf is to control, not kill its adversary. This is true of most single-dog attacks. Like the wolf, its mindset is to control, not kill. It's only when the controlling morphs into defending, because the dog's adversary fights back, that fatalities often occur from single-dog attacks. On the other hand, when wolves attack as a group, the mindset of the group is to kill, not control, whatever it is they are attacking. Because of this, when you are under attack from more than one dog of substantial size and power, you will most likely be dealing with animals intent on killing you, not trying to control you. Consequently, employing the defensive strategy used for single-dog attacks, such as not fighting back and playing dead, is most often ineffective. In 2015 alone, four children under the age of 7 years old, and three adults over the age of 79, were killed in multi-dog attacks. In each case, the victim was either too young or too old to fight back, and once they were pulled to the ground, any threat they had posed to the attacking dogs should have been neutralized and the attack should have ceased. Yet, the dogs continued their attacks and all of the victims were savagely mauled to death anyway. Again, when dogs attack in groups, the sole purpose of their attack is to kill their target, not neutralize it. Therefore, the best defense is a "no holds barred," determined-to-stay-alive-at-all-cost, offense.

If you do mount such an offensive attack, there is no guarantee that your tactic will work. In fact, if you are being assaulted by two or more powerful dogs, chances are that you'll probably be overpowered by them and receive severe injuries or be killed regardless. But what other choice do you have? Prevention has failed miserably, and escape is no longer an option. Your attackers are on you with the intent to kill you, and if you want to survive, your only chance will be to fight your way out. No matter how much you love dogs, you'll have to attack these dogs, because it's your life or theirs. And no matter what other dog lovers or animal rights groups might think of your actions, it's your life, not theirs. It's kill-or-be-killed time, which is no time to hold back. Attack!

When you attack, you will need to commit every resource you have to the fight and use anything and everything nearby as a weapon. When fighting for your life against multiple medium- to large- size dogs, whether you swing a lamp, broom, branch, or your fists at your attackers, swing for the fences. If you kick them, kick like a deranged mule. If you scream at them, send Hell from your lungs. If you claw them, dig in deep and tear something off. In this kind of fight, it won't be about damage control. It'll be about damaging your attackers as swiftly and as thoroughly as you can before they damage you. You'll have to convince your attackers that the cost of killing you is not worth the benefit. To even come close to succeeding, you'll have to temporarily vacate all of the endearing qualities of being a human, like grace and compassion, and become a savage animal instead. You will have to mount a relentless attack and keep attacking until you drive the dogs away, or you can't attack any longer. If the latter happens, curl up and cover up and pray.

Surviving the aftermath

I have survived multiple single dog attacks and two multi-dog attacks. As a consequence, I bear scars physically and emotionally, like most other victims. I am no longer able to grip as strongly with my left hand as I was able to prior to my last attack, when my forearm was severely damaged by a large German Shepherd. Before that attack, a Rottweiler had broken three bones in the same hand. My right shoulder aches constantly and sounds like tiny bubble wrap when it's popped every time I lift my right arm as a result of an attack from a giant Schnauzer. Every time I hike or run in the woods, I tense up whenever I hear dogs barking or I enter a clearing where a house or trailer sits; the aftermath of my near escape in Alabama. I am alive, but part of me is dead. No one survives a dog attack fully intact.

In dealing with their attacks, many victims seek professional help, while for some others, professional help comes too late. Many victims try to carry on with their lives and do their best to put their tragedies behind them, while others try to carry on after putting their loved ones in the ground. Dog attacks occur to individuals, and the subsequent aftermaths of their attacks are individual as well. But, as a whole, all of the victims I have known and interviewed chose one way to move forward together. For managing the effects of my attacks, I chose to learn from them and pass what I learned to others so that hopefully they wouldn't have to, and so did the other victims. After all, the best plan for dealing with the aftermath of a dog attack is to not need to deal with it at all.

I have counseled thousands of people about what they should do in the event that they were ever attacked by their dog or someone else's. All of those that were attacked afterwards followed the recommendations for their particular situation and survived with minimal injuries. As I stated previously, there is no orthodox method or absolutes when it comes to surviving single- or multi-dog attacks. The ones that I have included come from my knowledge and years of observing social predatory behavior and from my blood and experience, and that of thousands of other survivors of dog attacks. All of this serves as the foundation of the most important recommendation that I can make to crawl away or walk away from a dog attack. **Believe that you can.**

Attacks to Children - The Principle of Resemblance

In the wild, the physical size of a wolf allows the alpha pair to distinguish the difference between the cubs, adolescents, and young adults within their pack. Proper distinguishing is important because they are all treated differently. The cubs are given far more leniency by the alpha pair and are handled more delicately than the adolescent wolves, whose delinquent behavior is in turn tolerated far better than that of their older brothers and sisters, the young adults. This variance in treatment has more to do with the level of threat that each developmental period poses to the alpha pair's position, than with the physical ability of their offspring to withstand punishment. This is because there are no rank entitlements in the linear hierarchies of wolf packs. Every position, including the alpha pair, must be aggressively defended from the other members of the pack. And because wolf packs are forced to survive under conditions where there is often not enough food for all of its members, positions are constantly being challenged because it pays to have a position as near to the top of the totem pole as possible to ensure a higher chance of getting something to eat. As young adult wolves grow to two years of age, they develop in size and strength until they are nearly equal to that of their parents, and as a consequence they take on a more critical and threatening perspective by their parents who, in turn, adjust their conduct toward them in an attempt to maintain their top positions. In other words, if you're the alpha male, the day your oldest son can look you in the eyes without having to raise his head is the day you quit regarding him as your son and begin regarding him as your biggest and strongest opponent for the coveted top position you hold. Instinctually, you realize that should you ever stumble, your new opponent will not lend you a hand to help you get up. Instead, he will do his best to make sure you stay down as he passes you by. Therefore, if you wish to retain your number one position, you will have no choice but to either keep him squarely underneath your paw or send him packing. In most instances, he'll eventually leave on his own, but until then, you'll need to disregard any of your own grace, and any insubordination or challenges from him will have to be dealt with quickly and severely. It's nature's version of the **principle of resemblance**, and it's the reason why children are treated the same way as adults by dogs. When two-year old Timmy can finally look the two-year old family Doberman in the eyes without having to raise his head, he stops being a harmless "cub" to the Doberman. Instead, he becomes either an opponent or a threat, and he'll be treated like one should he ever try to take something from the Doberman or attack him with the remote-control device he snatched off the coffee table.

Most parents harbor the erroneous belief that if they acquire a puppy when their child is a baby, the two will grow up together and form an inseparable, human-like bond in which the dog will become the child's favorite playmate and comforter all wrapped up in a four-legged package. In addition, they also believe that because of the special bond that will come to exist between the two, the dog will assume a big brother or big sister attitude toward their child, and that not only will it never harm the child, it'll defend the child with its life to keep it from being hurt by someone else. Some parents will skip the hardships associated with rearing a puppy and a baby all at the same time and will elect to adopt an older dog instead. In doing so, they still assume many of the same beliefs as those of parents who acquire puppies for their children. The only difference is that they've simply taken a shortcut to the relationship both sets of parents want their dogs to have with their children: one that will always be filled with love, entertainment, and protection. In some cases, this dream relationship works out perfectly. However, in many, because of nature's principle of resemblance, it doesn't, and their children are bitten by the family dog.

As stated in the previous chapters, dogs, regardless of their size, will attack people for various reasons, regardless of the size of the person they're attacking, but it's usually the behavior of the individual, not their size, that forces the assault. Be that as it may, when a dog runs a possible human threat or competitor through a threat matrix or a cost versus benefit analysis because of their behavior, the physical size of the person (principle of resemblance) will factor greatly into their decision to attack or not. It will also factor into the level of violence that will be applied to any aggression they may use should they decide to attack. In the chapter titled "The Four Stages of Competitive Aggression," I used a story about one of the dogs belonging to me and my wife to describe the cost versus benefit analysis that dogs apply when defending high-value food and objects from perceived competitors. In the story, both my wife and I approached our dog, a small Maltese-Yorkie mix, who was defending a chocolate Hershey bar he had found, with the intent to take his prize from him. She is 5 feet, 7 inches tall.

I am 6 feet, 2 inches tall. In her attempt to take the bar, she was forceful. In my attempt, I was equally forceful. She got bitten. I got the Hershey bar. No doubt the obvious size difference between my wife and I played a major role in in the small dog's decision-making and the subsequent differing outcomes. For that reason, in comparison to the physical size of the defending dog, humans that are smaller than the dog (typically crawling babies or very small toddlers) are usually perceived as non-threats and lesser competitors for high-value food or objects. Therefore, the dog almost always elects to defend its food/object when challenged by them, but in such cases, if aggression is used, the dog will most often use a lighter, "easy win" level of competitive aggression versus what it would use against a larger, more capable human. On the other hand, humans that are head-level or greater in size than the defending dog (toddler - adult) can be perceived as serious threats and competitors and, as a result of this and other contributing factors, receive a mixed response to their interaction with the dog. The dog may choose to defend or give up the high-value food/object it possesses to the larger human, and likewise, it may choose to attack or flee from them if it feels that its safety is being threatened. In the event that the dog chooses to attack in either instance, the level of aggression it'll use against the larger human will always be above and beyond the level it would use against a human smaller than it. Therein lies the problem. By the time most children can pull themselves to an upright position or walk, they are either head-level or taller than most dogs. Overnight, because of the principle of resemblance, they suddenly transform from cub to young adult, from non-threats to threats, and from "easy wins" to capable competitors, and the resultant level of aggression that is applied to their status change is more than they can bear. In a twelve-year period spanning from 2005 to 2016, children between the ages of 0-9 made up 49% (193) of all dog bite fatality victims and approximately 4 million were treated at Emergency rooms.[25] To make matters worse, nearly 50% of the fatalities and injuries were caused by the family dog(s).

With regard to competitive, territorial, or self-defense aggression, children are not handled more delicately or given more leniency by dogs. If, for example, a young boy had been dancing on the same gravel road under the same harvest moon on the same night as Earl May, he would have received no special consideration by Pete and Boss for his age. They would have killed him as surely as they killed Earl May. If a young boy, instead of a middle-aged man, had violated the evolutionary rule of MINE by trying to take Cooper's prize bone, he would have been mauled by Cooper and found dead on the same kitchen floor as William Monroe. If a young girl had opened the door to Bo's Garage, instead of the adult woman that did, she would have been run down and killed by Brutus, Rambo, and Tiger before she would have gotten within ten yards of the truck window that was smashed by Sara McAlister's head when Brutus hit her like a runaway freight train. And, if a young girl had jumped on the same dog that had just killed three-year old Chloe over a piece of cheese, she would have been attacked the same as Marion Montgomery, but because of her smaller size, her body would not have been able to survive the thrashing that Marion sustained. Lastly, had an eight-year old boy wondered into the same backwoods settlement I did in rural Alabama, and been attacked by the same dogs, he would have never been seen again.

Dogs don't see harmlessness in children that are equal to or larger than them in size. The principle of resemblance, which is older than mankind and his children, won't allow it because visual size has always been a major component of the threat matrix and the competitive analysis that has been utilized by wolves to accurately distinguish friends from foes and opponents from non-opponents, and both were passed to our dogs. Size forces the individual wolf or dog to see potential competitors, trespassers, and threats in all other individual wolves and dogs of similar size, and it gives them the clearance to swing the "Hammer" against them as hard as they need to survive any encounter with them. Therefore, dogs will never judge the actions of a child by their age. Instead, they will be judged by their size, and the larger they are, the harder the "Hammer" will swing against them should their behavior warrant it. The sooner we come to grips with that reality and quit sacrificing our children for the sake of our anthropomorphic fantasies, the safer our children will become. Welcome to nature's version of the principle of resemblance. It can't afford to fantasize about anything because it must deal with kill-or-be-killed in the very real here-and-now existence.

When we accept the reality of the principle of resemblance, we will become more watchful of our children's actions around dogs. We will make sure they never violate the evolutionary rule of MINE, even if the object the family dog has in its mouth is their toy. We will also never take for granted that an unfamiliar dog will accept our children as a friend instead of a foe and allow them to walk unaware into a dog's critical zone and touch it. We will become the good zoo keepers that we should be by physically restraining our dogs when our family and friends' children breech the "invincible center" until our dogs prove they accept them. As our children grow, we will teach them about the natural mechanisms that govern canine behavior and how those mechanisms can cause their "best friend for life" to misinterpret their good intentions as bad ones, and how their friend might react accordingly in an aggressive manner. Soon, our children will come to respect but not fear the extremely predictable animal that has woven itself into the very fabric of our American culture, and they will learn how to conduct themselves when in its presence so as to never provoke an attack from it. Over time, they will do the same for their children, and they for theirs, and if the trend continues, there may come a time when the "Hammer" will swing against children no more.

Preventing attacks to children

Preventing dog attacks to children is not difficult. It just requires a completely different mindset than the one that has been responsible for hundreds of fatalities and millions of injuries to children so far, and the implementation of supervision and sound judgment once our mindset has changed. To accomplish this, we must pretend that our children are adults, because dogs won't pretend. We must always supervise their activities when in the company of a dog and make sure that they never do anything to them that you as an adult wouldn't do after reading this book. If our children cannot be supervised, we must become good zoo keepers and physically restrain our dogs in ways that they cannot harm our children. It's that simple. Keep it that way, because making it harder will make it harder for children to avoid being attacked by dogs.

The Impenetrable Lie

When creating social predators like wolves, nature made sure that she balanced the power of her creation in an effort to blunt aggression. Otherwise, if all wolves had been created equally powerful, they would have annihilated each other by now. Therefore, to prevent that from happening, she fabricated two different versions of wolves as part of her stable strategy: one being strong, confident, and possessing the drive to lead the other one being weaker, less secure, and driven more to follow. Both versions were combined, and the result was a relationship that mutually benefited from each other's excessive and lesser abilities.

A very long time ago, wolves came into contact with humans, who took note of the two versions and their respective pros and cons in regard to which version would make a better hunter and protector, and which would make a better worker and companion. They discovered that the stronger, more confident version made for great hunters and protectors, while the weaker, insecure version made for more cooperative workers and safer pets. Sometime later, some wolves turned into dogs and the two versions were duplicated so they could serve both wolf and dog. Humans soon began to grow and gather more food than they hunted and dogs who could work or serve as pets became the priority over hunting and protecting dogs. Over time, as machines developed, working dogs suffered the same fate as hunting and protecting dogs and found themselves being replaced by more and more companion dogs. As human populations became denser, some companion dogs became smaller and weaker so they could coexist safely and conveniently with millions of humans. Soon, even that wasn't enough, because some of the humans became weaker and more insecure than their weak and insecure companions and set about trying to correct the situation by making an even weaker and more insecure animal than the ones they had. Eventually they succeeded, and now, some dogs are born so genetically weak, they are predisposed at birth to become irrationally fearful of just about anything or anyone.

As these types of dogs grow and develop, their fearful predisposition worsens and their existence becomes one of perpetual stress. In time, the stress attacks their minds and paranoia sets in. They start seeing threats where threats don't exist. Every encounter becomes a foe, never a friend. Soon afterwards, aggression becomes their coping mechanism until someone is unjustifiably attacked and the dog is euthanized. But long before the fateful attack occurs and the dog is euthanized, the dog could have been saved with a proper pharmacotherapy program that involved the use of human-grade antidepressants and deactivation training. Here's how it works:

If a dog were to detect a possible threat, such as the approach of an unfamiliar person displaying antagonistic behavior, its physiological response to the threat would be the immediate preparation of all physical resources for fight or flight, should either become necessary. Information concerning the threat (e.g. species, size, location, movement, communication signals, etc.) would be passed from the dog's visual, auditory, haptic, and olfactory sensors to the amygdala (emotional processing part of the brain/warning center) where the information would be interpreted and assigned a high, medium, or low-risk value. Medium to high risks would cause the amygdala to send an alert to the hypothalamus (brain command center). Upon receiving the alert, the hypothalamus would send a signal to the adrenal glands, which would respond by releasing the hormone adrenaline into the dog's bloodstream. The sudden surge of adrenaline would cause the dog's body to release stored glucose (energy) into the bloodstream to provide fuel for its muscles. When this happened, the dog's breathing and heart rate would immediately accelerate. Smaller airways in the lungs would then open to allow for extra oxygen, which would be added to the fast-flowing blood carrying stored fuel to all of the dog's muscles and vital organs. As a result, the dog's senses would heighten and it would become extremely alert. Its muscles, full of oxygenated blood and fuel, would twitch in preparation for battle or for taking flight. All of this would occur faster than the perceived threat could advance one step closer.

Should the threat not advance one step closer, but instead remain where it was and continue with its antagonistic behavior, the dog's brain would continue to receive danger signals until the threat went away. Until that occurred, to ensure that the life-saving adrenaline does not dissipate, the hypothalamus would release corticotrophin-releasing hormones (CRH), which would cause the release of adrenocorticotropic hormones (ACTH), which would cause the adrenal glands to release cortisol, a steroid hormone that would keep the dog alert and ready to do battle or take flight. When the threat finally goes away, the cortisol levels in the dog's bloodstream would lower, and the dog's physiological state would return to normal.

Does this sound familiar? It should, because our bodies respond the same way. Nature gave dogs and us extra help swinging the "Hammer" and a little more pep to our step should we elect to drop the "Hammer" and run. No doubt, her gift has contributed to both of our species' ability to stay alive when the chips are down, and for that, we should be thankful. However, like any good gift, if it's given too often, it quits being a gift and starts becoming a nuisance. Such is the case when life-sustaining adrenal hormones like cortisol are released too often due to pathological stress. Over a period, the continued increase in cortisol levels in the bloodstream begin to harm the individual dog or human so much so that it has been implicated in shortened life spans, gastrointestinal issues, suppressed immune systems, reproduction failure, and, more importantly, brain dysfunction. This happens because cortisol slowly diminishes the chemicals that brain cells use to communicate with each other (neurotransmitters), with serotonin and dopamine being affected the most. Serotonin is commonly referred to as "happy juice" because it positively affects our mood, and dopamine is known as "motivational juice" because it is the chemical that gives us that extra push to get going when we need it. When both are depleted by a continuous assault from corticosteroids, brain cells are unable to communicate effectively, and then mood and motivation both take a severe downward turn. With dogs, this condition creates a perpetual, unwarranted state of fear and anxiety that blurs the line between valid threats and non-threats, and friendly behavior and not-friendly behavior. As a consequence, predictability flies out the window, and people suddenly find themselves being attacked by afflicted dogs for reasons that are not in character with normal canine aggressive behavior. It's a very dangerous condition that

I call **the impenetrable lie**. This is a condition where anything and anyone can be construed as a threat and anything you do to convince the stricken dog otherwise is considered a lie. Without proper treatment, these unwarranted fears become more acute as the dog ages and the aggressive behaviors that allowed the dog to cope with it are repeatedly reinforced. And no matter how much time, energy, and money you put into obedience training or desensitization programs, you won't be able to penetrate the lie unless you utilize a two-dimensional approach that involves blending psychoactive medications with a deactivation training program tailored for the dog's individual condition.

Dogs that suffer from stress-induced brain dysfunction are often treated the same as humans who suffer from a similar condition. Both are usually given antidepressants that generally function by restoring the balance of depleted neurotransmitters, like serotonin and dopamine, and as a result, brain cells are able to communicate effectively and mood and motivation are both enhanced. Once this is accomplished, therapy may or may not be used to adjust or deactivate any undesired behaviors that originated from the human's effort to cope with their condition. However, with dogs, even though a chemical benefit may also be achieved through the use of psychoactive medications, the addition of therapy is an absolute MUST for their successful rehabilitation. This is because in most cases, the maladaptive behavior created by the dog's attempt to cope with its condition has become fixed by the time most dog owners run out of excuses for their dog's aggressiveness and finally seek help! By fixed, I mean that the aggressive response to perceived threats reaches a reflexive state where attacks occur spontaneously and without provocation the moment the threat presents itself. For instance, when you encounter a red light while driving and talking on your cellphone at the same time, must you hang up and then consciously remove your foot from the gas pedal and then concentrate on how much pressure you apply to the brake pedal, or, are you able to keep chatting while your car seemingly stops itself? If your answer is the latter, it's because the color of the light that has always communicated to STOP your car has always been the same. It's always been RED. It's never been purple, blue, gray, or any other color. Therefore, when you see red, you stop your car. No need to take your mind away from your conversation. Your response to red lights while driving has become fixed. That's actually a good thing. But imagine if you moved to a country that required you to GO when the light turned red and stop when the light turned green? Now, all of a sudden, your fixed behavior is a bad thing and you would have to concentrate immensely on performing the correct behavior any time you encountered traffic lights. This is why therapy including deactivation training must be used in conjunction with psychoactive medications. Even if the psychoactive medication used in a pharmacotherapy program restores neurotransmitters levels to a normalized state, the dog's aggressive behavior when it encounters a previous trigger (unfamiliar human) will remain the same unless we force the dog to change its behavior. Otherwise, the only good thing that will occur with the administration of medication alone is that when people are bitten spontaneously and without provocation, at least they'll be bitten by a happy dog!

When performing pharmacotherapy with an aggressive dog, it is best to regard the medication being administered as only a temporary facilitator of the deactivation training that will cause the permanent change in the dog's behavior, so that you won't be tempted to utilize medication by itself.

If it helps, think of it this way: If you chose to enlighten a man on the values that embody Shakespeare's Hamlet while he was drowning in a pool, you would have chosen a very poor time to do so. Regardless, if you wished to continue with your endeavor, you would first have to pull the poor chap to the side of the pool and allow him to gather his wit and his wind. After he has done so sufficiently, you would stand a far better chance of him being receptive to your teachings, which would in turn allow you to impart the values of Shakespeare's Hamlet with some success. Any psychoactive medication used for canine rehabilitation purposes serves only to pull the poor dog to the side of the pool where it is able to gather its wit and its wind. When the dog has done so sufficiently, the deactivation training that will teach the dog how to climb out of the pool by itself in the event that it ever falls in again can proceed. On a more scientific level, the process starts like this:

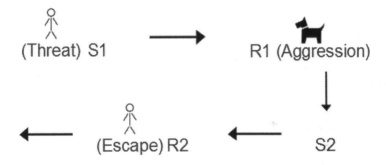

(Threat) S1 → R1 (Aggression)

← (Escape) R2 ← S2

In the diagram above, the dog sees a human. Because the dog suffers from a persistent, unwarranted fear that has created the illusion that all unfamiliar humans are threats, the human's presence alone (S1) is enough to communicate a threat to the dog. The dog reacts to S1 by acting aggressively (R1). The dog's aggressive response serves as a signal (S2) that is communicated back to the human - "DON'T COME CLOSER!" The human interprets the signal and becomes afraid. Not wishing to be bitten by the dog, the fearful human responds by going away from the dog (R2). The dog learns that its aggressive behavior achieves the desired result of repelling human threats, and with enough reinforcement, the behavior will become fixed.

To rehabilitate the dog, you would first have to administer the proper medication at the proper dosage that would be required to restore its neurotransmitters to normal levels. In most cases, antidepressants such as fluoxetine, clomipramine, amitriptyline, and trazodone are used with occasional augmentation from medications like clonidine and buspirone. Once the dog's brain chemical levels are restored, typically within 3-4 weeks after commencement of daily intake of the proper medication, the threshold requiring an aggressive response from the dog to known triggers (unfamiliar humans) will raise sufficiently enough for you to embark upon deactivating undesired fixed behaviors (aggression). In other words, after medicating the dog sufficiently, you will be able to work with an animal that will be very concerned about the presence of unfamiliar humans, but not terrified, and that's huge! A concerned animal is much more receptive to trying out different methods of making human threats go away than animals that are terrified! If you embark upon deactivation training and the dog you are trying to rehabilitate still panics when it sees strangers after it has been on a psychoactive medication for over 3-4 weeks, you will need to reevaluate the medication your using and the dosage that is being administered. Sometimes, you will have to change both to achieve the desired effect.

When embarking upon your deactivation program, your goal should be to teach the dog that aggression is not necessary to make human threats go away. This is accomplished by first preventing the dog's use of aggression, and then replacing it with a non-aggressive behavior. In time, the dog will learn that its non-aggressive behavior achieves the same results as its former aggressive behavior in that human threats continue to go away.

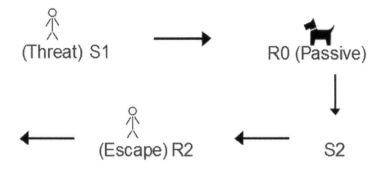

(Threat) S1 $\longrightarrow$ R0 (Passive)

(Escape) R2 $\longleftarrow$ S2

In the diagram above, the dog sees an unfamiliar human (S1). But because the dog has been on a proper psychoactive medication for 3-4 weeks, the threat level has now dropped from high- to medium- to low-risk level, allowing the dog to be receptive to its owner's input. The dog's owner prevents the dog from utilizing his fixed response of aggression by commanding the dog to sit and be quiet instead, which creates a non-aggressive/passive response from the dog (R0). The dog's passive response serves as a signal (S2) that is communicated back to the human - "I AM UNDER CONTROL." The human interprets the signal and remains relaxed. The dog's owner instructs the human to not approach the dog because, at this point in the rehabilitation process, the human is still a threat, albeit a lesser threat, and any incursions by the unfamiliar human into the dog's critical zone could result in him or her still being bitten. The human obliges and walks away (R2). Bingo! The dog learns that acting aggressively no longer works for repelling human threats, but sitting and being quiet does! With enough reinforcement, the passive response will become fixed. Plus, there's a bonus. In the first diagram, the human threat became fearful when the dog acted aggressively. That fear added to the dog's fear, causing the entire encounter to become more terrifying, and as a result, the dog's aggression escalated. In the second diagram, however, the human threat relaxed when the dog sat and became quiet. The human's calmness was then sensed by the dog, who also remained calmer because of it, and the result was a de-escalation, not an escalation, of aggression!

Pharmacotherapy can also be used to help dogs overcome phobias, obsessive compulsive behaviors, and separation anxiety, but regardless of what it's used for, the process remains similar in that you apply medicine + wait 3-4 weeks + evaluate chemical effect of medicine + deactivate undesired behavior while still giving medicine + taper off current dosage + evaluate results. Rehabilitation requires six months to a year to complete for most dogs, with the length of time the dog suffered from its condition before medicinal intervention occurred and the depth of the fixed undesired behavior as the major determining factors. Ultimately, no dog should have to remain on a psychoactive medication for longer than a year, and definitely not for life. That's because once the new response to the known trigger becomes fixed, it'll stay that way for better or worse unless something forces the dog to change its behavior. Plus, as a sort of ripple effect, the dog's new behavior usually receives positive reinforcement from the stimulus that used to terrify it or cause it to be anxious. For instance, dogs that ignored bones and other toys while they chewed themselves bloody raw because their OCD condition drove them to do so suddenly find pleasure in chewing bones and toys, and their bodies don't hurt any longer. Dogs that could not bear to be separated from their owners find themselves utilizing the peace and quiet of an empty house to take an extra nap or two. Most importantly, aggressive dogs that act calm in the presence of unfamiliar humans receive calm and friendly behavior from the unfamiliar humans in return, and therefore, most strangers stop being threats to the dog. When you cast a stone into a pond you're certain to get ripples, and a stone called pharmacotherapy creates the best.

It's a shame that our selfish manipulation of a once-flawless creature has led to some dogs suffering from the harmful effects of pathological stress; as if living in an alien world wasn't stressful enough for them. For these types of dogs, every act of kindness by a stranger is a lie. Every smile, every reach to pet, and every affectionate word is just one big lie. If you believe that you own such a dog but think the problem will go away on its own, that's an even bigger lie. And should your dog kill or seriously injure someone because their mere presence was enough to provoke an attack by your stricken dog, their safety is the biggest lie of all. Don't live your life with your dog as a lie. If it needs professional help, get it. But be sure that the help you get is well-versed in the two-dimensional approach of medicine and therapy combined, because that is the only way to penetrate the impenetrable lie.

The Hammer Falls

As I watched from my concealed blind, a wolf cautiously approached the large moose haunch that I had laid on the other end of an extensive clearing, across from where I was hiding. Even from where I sat, a good hundred yards away, the rank smell of the rotting meat was overpowering; but because I could smell it, it meant the wind was blowing in my direction, and that meant that as long as I didn't make a sound, I stood a good chance of not being detected by the wolf. Before winter, I had scouted the area looking for wolf signs, and I had just about given up finding anything when I had come across several sets of prints heading in opposite directions through the clearing that the moose haunch was currently lying in. All of the prints meant the area was either heavily trafficked by an individual pack, or a rival pack had decided to embark on an extra-territorial foray. Either way, it was the best place I had been able to find to risk using a $200 moose haunch for the sake of luring in wolves for observation.

The wolf hadn't fully committed to exposing itself for the free meal, so all I could make out through my binoculars was part of its torso, which was enough for me to know that the winter had not been kind to it. The outline of its rib cage was exposed by the ultra-thin hide covering it, and two of the ribs appeared to be misshapen under a crisscross of scars and missing fur. While waiting for the wolf to make its next move, I slowly glassed the surrounding area to see if it had brought any company along for the ride. If the wolf had, I didn't want any of the others sneaking up on me, which was possible because wolves often send scouts around the perimeter of clearings to look for any hint of danger or possible human incursions before exposing themselves. I knew I had been careful not to leave a trace of my presence, but sometimes with wolves you don't have to leave a trace to be found out anyway. The little voice in each of us that occasionally whispers a warning of possible danger when our other senses say otherwise is much keener in the wild. I once observed a female wolf from several miles away suddenly stop in her tracks and stare up into the boughs of a tall pine tree where the camouflaged surveillance video camera that was allowing me to watch her every move rested. The video camera had been strategically placed in a location that allowed it to view a vast expanse of forest floor, but it was impossible to be seen from the wolf's vantage point. Yet, somehow, she knew she was being watched. As she continued to stare, her eyes narrowed until their brilliant amber hue was replaced with only the black of her pupils showing through their tiny slits. Staring back at the monitor, I found myself holding my breath. As ridiculous as it seems, I honestly felt that at the time, she was looking at me. Then, at the moment that I could hold my breath no longer, she vanished.

MINE! The roar of the growl jerked me back to the present and startled me so badly, I gasped and reflexively reached for the Colt .45 auto holstered on my right hip. Being as deep as I was in wolf and bear territory by myself required knowing what you could find yourself up against at any moment, a sound plan for dealing with it, and a whole lot of luck to make it out of the area in the same shape you came in with. If any of that failed, that's when the .45 auto would come in handy. While my right hand rested on the pistol's grip, my other hand quickly moved the binoculars around the edge of the clearing to locate the source of the growl. Scanning from left to right, I concentrated on the dark areas that were ten feet off of the perimeter, looking for the obvious danger that lurked in the shadows.

MINE! Another roar from the area next to the foul-smelling moose haunch! I abandoned my scan of the shadows and whipped the binoculars to the right. The emaciated wolf that I had partially observed approaching the moose haunch earlier was now fully exposed and straddling the meat. It was slightly angled away from me, and all of its attention was directed to one of the dark areas I had just glassed. MINE! The roar came again, and I suddenly found myself having to release the pistol grip and grab the binoculars with both hands to keep it steady. The thumping of my heart had become so loud, I feared it would give me away at any second. I had heard the menacing growl of wolves many times in the past, and it had always been unsettling, but there was something about the sound coming from this wolf that had me unnerved like no other time. My mind was racing to figure out what it was when a flicker of movement came from the shadows that held the wolf's attention. I turned the center focus knob on my binoculars to pull more detail from the dark recess behind the trees that were in front of the wolf. After a few minute adjustments, I caught the source of the movement and the reason for the wolf's sudden aggression. It was two other wolves. Both were much larger than the emaciated wolf straddling the meat. Their chests were broad, and muscles rippled all throughout their forms as they weaved, undecidedly, among the trees. These wolves had weathered the deep snow and subzero temperatures of winter much better than the other wolf. It was clear now that they weren't the company I had been worried about. Instead, they were the competition, and by the looks of their size and their coordinated movements, it was not going to be much of one. And as I watched, indecision turned into purpose, and the two wolves stopped their weaving and began their advance toward the sole defender of the meat they wanted.

MINE! The roar tore through the forest as the two wolves emerged from the shadows. Silently cursing myself for jumping again, I unholstered the .45 auto and laid it in my lap. A terrible fight was about to happen, and if it came my way, I wanted to be ready. The echo of the previous roar had just faded when another came again, but deeper and more sinister than the one before. The two rival wolves, seemingly unfazed by the vocal threat emanating from their adversary, continued their march toward the prize that they believed would soon fill their stomachs. As they drew closer, I focused on the unwavering stare being given by the larger of the two wolves. It was ruthless, but without malice. And it held no disrespect for the haggard defender who was trembling and panting from the strain of its growling and holding its body taut, for hunger knows no respect. Neither did it hold compassion or a willingness to share, for hunger knows not what sharing is either. Instead, what it held was a single-purpose intent: Take the food.

Turning my attention back to the gaunt wolf defending the moose haunch, I couldn't help but feel sorry for it. Its tail was tucked between its legs, and its body was shaking violently as its sides heaved from the exertion of making itself appear to be as threatening as it could. I had seen the look before and knew that it was born from a desperation that few of us will ever experience. And, as quick as that, I found myself rooting for it and hoping the two obviously better-off wolves would leave it alone and let it eat the meat. But even faster than that, reality squashed my altruistic hopes when the two better-off wolves charged and all Hell broke loose!

After what seemed like an eternity, I lowered my binoculars. My heart had stopped pounding, and my hands no longer shook as I watched the forest shadows encircle the clearing. With each passing minute, they tightened their grip, until the clearing was no more. In the dark, I could still hear the moose haunch being torn apart, and the occasional sounds of smaller predators rustling through the undergrowth as they waited impatiently for anything that might be left for them. It had been an epic battle that had been waged on two fronts: the right to eat and the right to stay alive. Both the attackers and the defender were blameless for their actions because it had been within their right to stake claim to the meat and to harm each other if it was needed to protect their claim. It had also been within their right that if harm were inflicted by any of them, the recipient of the harm would be allowed to use harm to defend themselves. Alas, the harm had been needed, and both attackers and defender had inflicted all that they could until one had inflicted more than the other and ended up with the meat.

None of that surprised me at the time, because that's how it is in the wild. No politics, no diplomacy, no hidden agendas, no waging war from a distant computer, and no BS. From where I was sitting, everything was up close and personal, and the "Hammer" falls hard on someone every time the agenda involves food acquisition, territorial defense, and self-defense; and the "Hammer" had fallen hard on a few wolves today. Therefore, I wasn't surprised that blood had been spilled for the precious meat. I also wasn't surprised by the outcome of the fight. After all, desperation knows no limits. Nor was I surprised when the emaciated winner paused from gorging itself long enough to give a good hard look in my direction to let me know that it had been aware of my presence the entire time! Even when I noticed the stare coming from two blue eyes I still wasn't surprised, but I should have been, because mature wolves don't have blue eyes. Nevertheless, it didn't surprise me because the "Hammer" that had allowed it to keep the food it so desperately needed and to fight off two adversaries that were trying to kill it wasn't given just to wolves.

Bibliography

1   Preventing Dog Bites, The Centers for Disease Control and Prevention, May 2015.

2   Plastic Surgery Statistics Report by the American Society of Plastic Surgeons, 2015.

3   Dog Bite Liability by Insurance Information Institute, 2016.

4   American Bar Association, Criminal and Civil Cases Involving Dog Attacks, 2010-2015.

5   Estimated U.S. Cities, Counties and Military Facilities with Breed-Specific Laws, DogsBite.org, 2016.

6   The Humane Society of the United States, Pets by the Numbers, Humansociety.org, APPA survey, 2015-2016

7   Societies of Wolves and Free-ranging Dogs, Stephen Spotte, Ph.D., Cambridge University Press, 2012.

8   U.S. Dog Bite Fatalities, DogsBite.org 2016

9   U.S. Dog Bite Fatalities, DogsBite.org 2016

10 The American Journal of Forensic Medicine and Pathology-Volume 20(3), September 1999, pp 243-246 Dog Pack Attack: Hunting Humans Avis, Simon P. M.D. F.R.C.P.C

11   U.S. Dog Bite Fatalities-2016

12   Dog Bite Force: Myths, Misinterpretations and Realities, Canine Corner, Stanley Coren, Ph.D., F.R.S.C., May 17, 2010

13   12-Year U.S. Dog Bite Fatality Chart- 2005 to 2016 by Breed, Dogsbite.org, Feb 2017

14   On Human Aggression, Edward O. Wilson, Harvard University Press, Cambridge, MA, 1979 [abridged— 3020 words]

15   It's a Wolf-Eat-Wolf World in the Wilds of Alaska, Tim Mowry, Fairbanks Daily News-Miner, February 19, 2009.

16   U.S. Dog Bite Fatalities, DogsBite.org 2014

17   Dog Attacks On Mail Carriers Rise Again As Online Sales Boom, Hope Yen, Associated Press, Washington, April 10, 2017

18   Brief Overview of Dangerous Dog Laws, Charlotte Walden, Michigan State University College of Law, 2015

19   Dog Owner Liability for Bites: An Overview, Mary Randolph, J.D., Nolo.com

20   Traumatic Deaths from Dog Attacks in the United States, Pinckney, Lee; Leslie A. Kennedy Pediatrics, 69 (2): 193–6, University of Texas, February 1982

21   Socialization and Society, John A. Clausen, Boston - Little Brown and Company, 1968

22   Percent of Land Area. U.S. Census Bureau, March 04, 2015

23   George Washington to John Trumbull, Founders.Archives. gov/Documents/Washington/ 06-04-02-0120, June 25, 1799

24   Discussion Notes - Single Dog Metric, DogsBite.org

25   12-Year U.S. Dog Bite Fatality Chart - 2005 to 2016 Victims by Age Groups, DogsBite.org, Feb 2017

Appendix A:
Canine warning signals

Hard stare – head up - ears pulled back
fangs showing – ready stance -
bone in mouth – **competitive aggression**

Hard stare – ears pulled back
fangs showing – leaning against fence -
body elevated to increase size – **territorial aggression**

Fixed stare – body tense and leaning away from hand –
mouth slightly open – ears pulled back –
self-defense aggression

Head and tail up – body taut and leaning forward – ears erect and forward – hard stare – mouth closed – **alert, confident, may attack if you enter the dog's critical zone or trespass**

Head low – ears down – indirect stare – mouth slightly open and showing teeth – **fearful, may attack if you enter the dog's critical zone**

Head high – body taut – mouth closed –
ears pulled back – fixed, wide-eyed stare – **fearful,
may attack if child makes contact**

About the Author

Raised in Fairbanks, Alaska, Bryan Bailey grew to appreciate the wildness of the land and its abundant wildlife. In particular, he developed a fondness for the gray wolves that roamed the vast mountain ranges and forests near his home. Under the guidance of a Special Forces Survival Instructor, he spent years studying the social interactions of wolves in their packs and discovered that, beyond obvious physical similarities, there were also behavioral similarities between the wolves and the sled dogs that were his family's pets.

Today, with over thirty five years of education and experience studying the natural mechanisms that govern the many uses of aggression by wolves, Bryan has become a Master at understanding how those same mechanisms, passed from the wolf, continue to influence the behavior of modern dogs and why they attack humans. Utilizing what he has learned, Bryan educates thousands of dog owners each year on the causes of dog aggression and how they can prevent from becoming a victim of it. By doing so, Bryan has been credited with saving hundred's of lives.

Bryan and his wife, Kira, live on the banks of the Mississippi River in Memphis, TN, with their children, dogs and cats. Together they own Taming the Wild, WILD DOGS and HOWL - The Way Home for Fearful and Aggressive Dogs.